THE
GOD WHO
SPEAKS TO
MAN

EXAMS TO: JOHN PLASTERER
BCDC CHAPLAIN'S OFFICE
OR MAIL TO
BALT SCHOOL OF BIBLE
1712 PARK AVE BALT MD 21217

ECS
MINISTRIES
The Word to the World

Developed as a study course by Emmaus Correspondence School, founded in 1942.

Published By:
ECS Ministries
PO Box 1028
Dubuque, IA 52004-1028
United States of America

Revised 2004
Reprinted 2006

ISBN 0-940293-81-1

Printed in United States of America.

INTRODUCTION

Welcome to your study of this course! This course is designed to help you think through for yourself great truths revealed by God for all mankind. You will examine their scope and significance and how they relate to you as a rational, thinking person.

Some of the concepts will no doubt be new to you. For this reason you will find them challenging. At the same time, because they are new to you they will, perhaps, cause you to think deeply about the issues involved.

You should not try to go through this book too quickly. This is a course to be studied. Tests are provided to help you evaluate your progress. Your instructor will grade these exams for you and will help you. He will endeavor to answer any questions which arise out of your studies.

LESSONS YOU WILL STUDY

- The Authority of the Bible
- What Is God Like?
- What Is A Prophet?
- The Continuity of Doctrine
- Prophecies Concerning Christ
- Why the Messiah Came
- The Most Important Question of All
- The Final Messenger
- The Sin Question
- Salvation From Sin
- Religion or Salvation
- Living the Life

HOW TO STUDY

You will notice that two typefaces are used in the body of the text. The portions in *italics* are quotations from the Bible. You should know how to find these passages (and the many others referred to in the text) in your Bible. Here is how to locate Bible passages from Scripture references. In the text, verses from the Bible are given with the name of book, chapter and verse. To find a verse, first look up the name of the book in the list at the beginning of the Bible. This will tell you at what page the book is found. Most books are divided into chapters, each about a page in length. The chapter is divided into verses, each about one sentence. For example, suppose you want to find 1 Peter 1:18. There are two books written by Peter so you must find the page number for the first book of Peter. The teaching you want is in chapter one and verse 18.

Begin by asking God to open your heart to receive the truths He would teach you form His Word. Read the lesson material through at least twice, once to get a general idea of the contents and then again slowly, looking up all the Scripture references.

EXAMS

There is an exam for each lesson. Each exam is clearly marked to show you which questions deal with which lesson. These exams can be found in the separate Exam Booklet. The entire exam booklet is to be sent back for grading when you have completed the course. After they are graded, the exams will be returned to you.

WHAT DO YOU SAY QUESTIONS

Questions headed in this way are designed so that you may freely state your own opinions in answer to the question. Your candid answers will help your instructor get to know you better as an individual. They will also help us evaluate the general effectiveness of this course.

HOW YOUR PAPERS ARE GRADED

Your instructor will mark any incorrectly answered questions. You will be referred back to the place in the Bible or the textbook where the correct answer is to be found. Upon completion of this study, you will receive a certificate showing your final grade.

GROUP ENROLLMENTS

If you are enrolled in a class, submit your exam booklet to the leader or secretary of the class who will send them for the entire group to the School.

GENERAL INSTRUCTIONS

Begin studying immediately, or, if you are in a group, as soon as the group begins. Try to keep a regular schedule. Many students endeavor to complete at least one lesson each week and take a maximum of one year to complete the course. We highly recommend the adoption of a regular study schedule.

CHAPTER ONE

THE AUTHORITY OF THE BIBLE

THE UNIQUENESS OF THE BIBLE

The Bible is unique! It is not enough to say that it is a unique Book, for it is a collection of sixty-six ancient Books. Moreover, this unique collection of Books is bound together by a central theme and a unity of purpose which makes the books into One Book.

This Book tells of the ways in which God revealed Himself to mankind over a period of several thousand years. This account of the ways in which God has intervened in human history provides us with a description of the nature and the attributes of God completely different from the concept of God found anywhere else in the entire world of literature. The Bible is history, but history strikingly different from ordinary history. Secular history tells of the rise and fall of nations, of great wars and battles, and of the ways in which men and nations have affected the peoples of surrounding territories. But the Bible goes further than that. The Bible is an interpretation of history, showing how men (as individuals and as nations) have either been blessed or punished by God for their attitude to Him and His holy laws. It is this unique explanation of the moral and spiritual factors behind the historical narrative, which makes the Bible so relevant to us today.

The Bible enables us to discover the will of God for our lives because this divine will is made plain in hundreds of real-life illustrations in the Bible. This is why we invite you to commence this study with us. We sincerely hope you will discover for yourself the truth about God Almighty, as Creator, Provider and Savior of men.

First, we must answer some of the questions many people have in their minds as they begin to read the Bible. Some say, for example, "Why should I read a book which is merely Jewish mythology?" Jewish mythology is quite different from what we find in the Bible. In fact the truth of the Bible will be quite evident to us as we continue our study. Others ask, "How could such an ancient Book still be relevant?" True, people today are much better educated than ever before; yet the Bible (in part or the whole) ranks as the "world's best-seller." Every year more than one hundred million copies are sold! So, when you read the Bible you are in good company, for millions of modern people are reading it! Moreover, it is not being read only by people in Western lands! The Bible (either in part or the whole) is being read today in more than twelve hundred languages. The Bible is being sold today in the languages of 97% of the world's population and is being read in almost every country and island on earth. For this reason alone, no person is really educated if he has not studied the most widely read Book in the literature of the world.

You will find a copy of the Bible helpful as a textbook for use with this course. Have you got a Bible beside you now? The first thing that impresses most beginners is the size of the Bible—it contains more than 800,000 words. Most people hardly know where to begin! Well, let us begin at the very beginning! Open your Bible at the title page and you will find an index listing the names of the sixty-six Books of the Bible. Notice there are two major divisions, one called the Old Testament and the other called the New Testament; both sections are divided into many subsections. In a later lesson we shall explain in detail what these two "Testaments" are and how they relate to each other. The Old Testament was written in the Hebrew language (except for a few small sections written in Chaldee) and the New Testament was written in the Greek language, which had become at that period the international language just as English is today.

The Old Testament begins with a concise account of the creation of the world. This unique narrative begins in the undated past, and records how God the Almighty Creator prepared the world, stage-by-stage, to be a home for mankind. When all was ready, God created man. From this logical beginning, the story continues for thousands of years until we reach the end of the Old Testament in the days of Malachi about 400 B.C. The New Testament covers a relatively short period from the birth of Jesus to the death of the Apostles. It was completed about 100 A.D.

THE AUTHORITY OF THE BIBLE

People must have a true and authoritative basis for their faith. Many popular religions are based entirely on human ideas and thus are merely theories or philosophies. Christianity is based on the Bible which Christians accept as their final authority because they believe it to be inspired by God. Thus, our first topic for study is the basis for this belief. Why do Christians believe the Bible to be a Book inspired by God? Our answer is found in the Bible itself.

1. THE BIBLE CLAIMS TO BE A REVELATION OF GOD.

This claim is found in a large number of places in the Bible. It is summed up in two short readings as follows:

> *Every scripture is inspired by God and useful for teaching, for reproof, for correction, and for training in righteousness, that the person dedicated to God may be capable and equipped for every good work* (2 Timothy 3:16–17).

> *No prophecy of scripture ever comes about by the prophet's own imagination, for no prophecy was ever borne of human impulse; rather, men carried along by the Holy Spirit spoke from God* (2 Peter 1:20–21).

These two short paragraphs give a definition of the Christian concept of the inspiration of Scripture. All Scripture is given by God. It was given in two main ways, first by **direct revelation** (by which the actual words of God are recorded by the prophets): second by **inspiration** (by which the Holy Spirit guided the prophets as they wrote and thus the prophets wrote Divine Truth). Let us examine these two aspects of the Divine origin of the Bible.

The Bible was given by means of **direct revelation.** Nearly four thousand times in the Bible we find words or expressions such as: *And God said . . .* or *The LORD spoke to Moses*, or *The Word of the LORD came to Isaiah.* You could look up the following references by way of example:

- God spoke to Moses (Exodus 3:4), about 1500 b.c.

9

- God spoke to Samuel (1 Samuel 3:11), about 1000 B.C.
- God spoke to Elijah (1 Kings 21:17), about 900 B.C.
- God spoke to Isaiah (2 Kings 20:1), about 700 B.C.
- God spoke to Jeremiah (Jeremiah 1:2), about 600 B.C.
- God spoke to Ezekiel (Ezekiel 1:3), about 600 B.C.
- God spoke to Malachi (Malachi 1:1–2), about 400 B.C.

The above dates are given in round numbers to convey the sense of historical continuity. Thus, God spoke directly to His prophets from time to time throughout the entire period of Israel's national existence commencing with Moses and ending with Malachi. These holy prophets received direct revelations from God and recorded them at His command. Thus, we have here the actual spoken Word of God.

The Bible was also given by means of the **inspiration of the Holy Spirit.** There are large sections of the Bible which contain history and poetry. Are these sections nothing more than Jewish literature? Certainly they are classified as Jewish literature, but even the Jewish people were able to distinguish between ordinary literature and Divinely inspired literature. "Direct revelation" from God was not necessary when the prophets were recording actual historical facts, but to be **authoritative** history it had to be inspired by God.

Because they were inspired by God, the prophets were divinely guided in the selection of **facts** to be written; they were divinely guided in the choice of **words** to describe the facts; and they were divinely guided in recording not merely human comment on the facts, but the **attitude of God** toward the behavior of the persons referred to. Thus by Divine inspiration, the prophets were protected from errors in historical fact, from errors in doctrine and from mistakes made through ignorance. In this way the Bible was kept from becoming a mixture of truth and legend which is what we find in most ancient books (for instance, the Greek classics). Modern research and archaeology have demonstrated the astonishing accuracy of Bible history and supports the claim that the Bible is inspired by God.

This briefly is what the Bible claims for itself. It is a Book (which, in some parts, is thousands of years old) which claims to be a record of the actual words of God to men, and of the ways in which He has dealt with men in history. Can such a claim be tested? Yes! In fact, God requires that we test this claim sincerely. About 2500 years ago, God spoke through the prophet Isaiah and challenged unbelievers to apply a very practical test. It is found in the following verses. Please read them carefully:

"Present your argument," says the LORD. "Produce your evidence," says Jacob's king. "Let them produce evidence! Let them tell us what will happen! Tell us about your earlier predictive oracles, so we may examine them and see how they were fulfilled. Or decree for us some future events! Predict how future events will turn out, so we might know you are gods. Yes, do something good or bad, so we might be frightened and in awe. Look, you are nothing, and your accomplishments are non-existent; the one who chooses to worship you is disgusting." (Isaiah 41:21–24).

"I am the LORD! That is my name! I will not share my glory with anyone else, or the praise due me with idols. Look, my earlier predictive oracles have come to pass; now I announce new events. Before they begin to occur, I reveal them to you." (Isaiah 42:8–9).

This is what the LORD, Israel's king, says, their protector, the LORD who leads armies: "I am the first and I am the last, there is no God but me. Who is like me? Let him make his claim! Let him announce it and explain it to me—since I established an ancient people—let them announce future events! Don't panic! Don't be afraid! Did I not tell you beforehand and decree it? You are my witnesses. Is there any God but me? There is no other protector; I know of none." (Isaiah 44:6–8).

"Remember what I accomplished in antiquity! Truly I am God, I have no peer; I am God, and there is none like me, who announces the end from the beginning and reveals beforehand what has not yet occurred, who says, 'My plan will be realized, I will accomplish what I desire,' who summons an eagle from the east, from a distant land, one who carries out my plan. Yes, I have decreed, yes, I will bring it to pass; I have formulated a plan, yes, I will carry it out" (Isaiah

46:9–11).

These verses clearly teach that the fact of inspiration and the facts of history when taken together will prove whether or not a prophet had written the words of God. One unique feature of the Bible is the vast amount of prophecy or prediction concerning future events it contains. God challenges men to examine these prophecies to see whether or not they have been fulfilled! For a prediction to be fulfilled in the way and in the time foretold by the prophet is proof that God spoke through the prophet. We will study this in detail in later lessons. This test can be applied to thousands of predictions in the Bible leading to the conclusion that God has spoken. The Bible's claim to be inspired by the Holy Spirit is the only possible answer to the amazing mystery of the foretelling of the future in accurate detail.

2. *THE AUTHORITY OF THE BIBLE DOES NOT DEPEND*
   ON OUR ABILITY TO UNDERSTAND IT.

Read the following verses:

Concerning this salvation, the prophets who predicted the grace that would come to you searched and investigated carefully. They probed into what person or time the Spirit of Christ within them was indicating when he testified beforehand about the sufferings appointed for Christ and his subsequent glory (1 Peter 1:10–11).

And regard the patience of our Lord as salvation, just as also our dear brother Paul wrote to you, according to the wisdom given to him (2 Peter 3:15).

You will notice that even the prophets themselves did not fully understand the words that God spoke through them or revealed to them. They were simply God's messengers, and often the great truths they wrote down were too profound for them to understand. No human mind can fully understand Divine truths. A Muslim leader once asked, "Would God punish a man for failing to understand Bible doctrines?" The answer is, "No, we are not punished because we cannot understand the mysteries of the Bible, but for unbelief—for refusing to believe what God has said." The prophets themselves were unable to understand the great truths they taught, so obviously many aspects of Divine revelation are beyond the limitations of our minds. This problem is partly explained by our next point.

3. DIVINE TRUTH CANNOT BE COMPRESSED INTO THE LIFE SPAN OF ANY HUMAN BEING.

Study this verse:

They [the Prophets] were shown that they were serving not themselves but you, in regard to the things now announced to you through those who proclaimed the gospel to you by the Holy Spirit sent from heaven—things angels long to catch a glimpse of. Therefore, get your minds ready for action by being fully sober, and set your hope completely on the grace that will be brought to you when Jesus Christ is revealed. (1 Peter 1:12–13).

God is eternal, and we are mortal. For this reason Divine revelation is progressive. God's promises and revelations began in the first era of human life on earth, and continued through the centuries with new aspects of truth being added from time to time. Predictions were fulfilled in some cases hundreds of years after they were made, and so the prophets did not live long enough to see the fulfillment of their own words. Some of the prophecies in the Bible will not be fulfilled until the coming day of judgment. It is foolish for a man to reject a revelation because it does not fit in with the local circumstances of his short life span. Faith in God compels us to believe that God's revelations embrace the entire period of His dealings with the human race. This is why we continually stress the vital need for clear historical perspective in our study of the Bible.

4. THE AUTHORITY OF THE BIBLE IS UNCHANGING AS THE SOURCE OF MORAL CONDUCT.

We see this in the verse we began with, 2 Timothy 3:16–17. Because the Bible is given by inspiration of God it is profitable. It teaches us the truth about God and states the kind of moral conduct God requires of us. It is profitable for doctrine, for instruction and for correction. For this reason, our study of the Bible cannot be treated simply as an academic exercise! Unless we are willing to obey God's Word with a sincere heart, we will never learn the deepest truths it contains about eternal life. When we read the Bible seriously and ask God to speak to our hearts through its inspired teachings, we begin to realize that God does indeed speak to men with Divine authority through His Word, the Bible.

CHAPTER TWO

WHAT IS GOD LIKE?

In the modern world, atheism is making a bold attempt to banish all thought of God from the minds of men. By teaching that men and apes evolved from a common ancestor, atheists try to prove that all ignorance, superstition, witchcraft and religion are related to man's primitive state. They blandly assume that science has banished all such ignorant beliefs and demand that God must be rejected along with fairies and goblins. Yuri Gagarin, the Russian cosmonaut, joked that up in space he saw no sign of God. What did he expect to see? Was his concept of "God" that of an old gentleman sitting on a cloud? But is God like that? What is God like?

THE BIBLE DOES NOT ATTEMPT TO PROVE THE EXISTENCE OF GOD

It does not need to, because it is in itself the record of the way God has revealed Himself to mankind. Thus it begins with a positive statement of the fact that there is a God and states that those who come to God must believe in Him. It says, *In the beginning God created the heavens and the earth* (Genesis 1:1). *Now without faith it is impossible to please him, for the one who approaches God must believe that he exists and that he rewards those who seek him.* (Hebrews 11:6).

The Bible begins with the statement that God is the Almighty Creator. The account of the creation of our world is found in Genesis 1:1–28. You should read this in your Bible. This short paragraph contains an implicit denial of all subsequent deviations from the truth about God. It refutes *atheism* which says there is no God. It refutes *polytheism* which says there are many gods. It refutes *pantheism* which says that the universe is "God." It refutes *humanism* which worships man himself. It refutes *astrology* which says that the stars affect destiny, whereas in fact they are only part of God's inanimate creation.

15

FROM THE BEGINNING OF HUMAN LIFE, MEN KNEW GOD

The evolutionary theory claims that because the primitive ape-man creatures were afraid of the forces of nature they began to imagine all kinds of unseen spirits and gods in their environment. As their knowledge increased they developed the "god idea" until eventually the concept of One God emerged. The Bible refutes this idea emphatically. Romans 1:18–25 says: *For the wrath of God is revealed from heaven against all ungodliness and unrighteousness of people who suppress the truth by their unrighteousness, because what can be known about God is plain to them, because God has made it plain to them. For since the creation of the world his invisible attributes—his eternal power and divine nature—have been clearly seen, because they are understood through what has been made. So people are without excuse. For although they knew God, they did not glorify him as God or give him thanks, but they became futile in their thoughts and their senseless hearts were darkened. Although they claimed to be wise, they became fools and exchanged the glory of the immortal God for an image resembling mortal human beings or birds or four-footed animals or reptiles. Therefore God gave them over in the desires of their hearts to impurity, to dishonor their bodies among themselves. They exchanged the truth of God for a lie and worshiped and served the creation rather than the Creator, who is blessed forever! Amen.* This very important statement shows plainly that, from the very beginning men knew God but they turned away from Him. Thus false religion and idolatry is not a primitive fear-concept, but a later development which arose when men deliberately exchanged truth for error.

From the beginning, God the Creator revealed Himself to man. God talked with Adam (Genesis 1:28), with Noah (Genesis 6:13), with Abraham (Genesis 12:1). You might wish to look up these references in your Bible and see what God said to them. Man's rebellion and disobedience has resulted in a distortion by him of the pure knowledge of the One True God. By the time of Abraham, idolatry was almost universal. God called Abraham to leave his own country with its idolatry and corrupt culture to journey to the land of

Canaan, where he was to found a new nation devoted to the worship of the One True God. Here is the record of that call: *So Abram left, just as the LORD had told him to do, and Lot went with him. (Now Abram was seventy-five years old when he departed from Haran.) And Abram took his wife Sarai, his nephew Lot, and all the possessions they had accumulated and the people they had acquired in Haran, and they left for the land of Canaan. They entered the land of Canaan. Abram traveled through the land as far as the oak tree of Moreh at Shechem. (At that time the Canaanites were in the land.) The LORD appeared to Abram and said, "To your descendants I will give this land." So Abram built an altar there to the LORD, who had appeared to him. Then he moved from there to the hill country east of Bethel and pitched his tent, with Bethel on the west and Ai on the east. There he built an altar to the LORD and worshiped the LORD.* (Genesis 12:4–8). The Divine plan of course, required a considerable period for its development. The family of Abraham first grew to be a tribe but by the time of Moses; it had become a nation.

THE FIRST WRITTEN LAWS CONCERNING THE WORSHIP OF GOD WERE GIVEN TO MOSES

At this point, please read the following verses:

I, the LORD, am your God, who brought you from the land of Egypt, from the house of bondage. You shall have no other gods before me. You shall not make for yourself a carved image or any likeness of anything that is in heaven above, or that is on earth under it, or that is in the water below. (Exodus 20:2–4).

Listen, Israel: The LORD is our God, the LORD is one. You must love the LORD your God with your whole mind, your whole being, and all your strength. (Deuteronomy 6:4–5).

Be very careful, then, because you saw no form at the time the LORD spoke to you at Horeb from the middle of the fire. I say this so you will not corrupt yourselves by making an image in the form of any kind of figure. This includes the likeness of a human male or female, any kind of land animal, any bird that flies in the sky, any insect on the ground, or any fish in the deep waters of the earth. When you look up to the sky, see the sun, moon, and stars—the whole heavenly creation—you must not be seduced to worship and serve them, for the LORD your God has assigned them to all the people of the world. (Deuteronomy 4:15–19).

These three paragraphs give the oldest and clearest statement of the Unity of God to be found anywhere in all the history of man. By the time of Moses (about 400 years after Abraham) the human race had so completely turned to the worship of false gods that it became necessary that the One True God should be clearly distinguished from the countless false gods and idols of the pagan world. That is why God, through Moses, revealed that His name was YAHWEH, (actually in Hebrew, only the consonants are given, as in Arabic script, so that the name of God appears as Y-H-W-H). In Exodus 3:15 we find the following words: *God also said to Moses, "You must say this to the Israelites, 'The LORD—the God of your fathers, the God of Abraham, the God of Isaac, and the God of Jacob—has sent me to you. This is my name forever, and this is my memorial from generation to generation.'"* Also in Exodus 6:2–3 we read: *God spoke to Moses and said to him, "I am the LORD. I appeared to Abraham, to Isaac, and to Jacob as God Almighty, but by my name 'the LORD' I was not known to them."* From this time onwards, the whole of the Old Testament plainly teaches that Yahweh is the One True God. Now read 1 Kings 18:39. The contest between the prophets of the pagan god Baal and Elijah the prophet of God was tremendous. The result was that the people cried out, *The LORD [Yahweh] is the true God! The LORD is the true God!* All other gods, by whatever name they were called, were false. Along with the revelation of the Name of God, there was given a strong safeguard to protect this great truth from corruption. Idols and images and "aids to worship" were completely forbidden. To keep this great truth alive God chose the people of Israel as His channel of Divine revelation—they were the "People of Yahweh, the people of the One True God." Unfortunately, they did not always maintain this privileged position, but often lapsed into idolatry themselves. For this God punished them repeatedly.

THE BIBLE REVEALS THE NATURE OF GOD BY WHAT HE DOES

The Bible purposely does not give a systematic description of what God is. Man is finite and cannot possibly understand a God who is infinite. Any description of God must therefore be inadequate. Because of this, God chose a way to reveal the mystery of His nature well within our grasp. He has revealed His nature by His acts. Thus the Bible is a written account of the way God has acted down the centuries.

1. GOD IN CREATION

The Bible tells us that the universe is the work of God. True science confirms this. With the telescope we study the immensity of space with its galaxies and star-systems or through the microscope we marvel at the intricate pattern of life scaled down to the minutest dimensions. We discover creatures so small they can find a mighty ocean in a single drop of water! We wonder at the exactness of natural laws, and at the miracle of design and beauty in every part of nature. We realize something of the greatness and the wisdom and power of the Creator. His work of creation teaches us that God is perfect in wisdom, intelligence and power.

2. GOD IN PROVIDENCE

Abraham is a classic example of God's love and care for the individual. God called him to obedience and faith, and in the constantly recurring crises of life, Abraham learned the reality of the love and care and provision of God. The whole story of Abraham (Genesis 12–25) is recorded for our benefit. Read it in your Bibles

3. GOD IN HISTORY

One of the ways the people of Israel recalled the greatness of God was by reciting what He had done in their national history. Psalms 78, 105 and 106 are good illustrations of this. Here is just one example taken from Psalm 78. Read this whole psalm in your Bible and look up the other two as well:

He did amazing things in the sight of their ancestors, in the land of Egypt, in the region of Zoan. He divided the sea and led them across it; he made the water stand in a heap. He led them with a cloud by day, and with the light of a fire all night long. He broke open rocks in the wilderness, and gave them enough water to fill the depths of the sea. He caused streams to flow from the rock, and made the water flow like rivers. Yet they continued to sin against him, and rebelled against the Sovereign One in the desert. They willfully challenged God by asking for food to satisfy their appetite. They insulted God, saying, "Is God really able to give us food in the wilderness? Yes, he struck a rock and water flowed out, streams gushed forth. But can he also give us food? Will he provide meat for his people?" When the LORD heard this, he was furious. A fire broke out against Jacob, and his anger flared up against Israel, because they did not have faith in God, and did not trust his ability to deliver them (Psalm 78:12–22).

Study **what God has revealed** about His own nature and His will, and compare the accounts of **what He has done.** You will find a thrilling combination of factors which display the glory of God. Here are a few of them:

God is One—*Listen, Israel: The LORD is our God, the LORD is one.* (Deuteronomy 6:4).

God is Living—*The LORD is the only true God. He is the living God and the everlasting King. When he shows his anger the earth shakes. None of the nations can stand up to his fury.* (Jeremiah 10:10).

God is Self-existing—*God said to Moses, "I AM that I AM." And he said, "You must say this to the Israelites, 'I AM has sent me to you.'"* (Exodus 3:14).

God is Eternal—*O sovereign Master, you have been our protector through all generations! Even before the mountains came into existence, or you brought the world into being, you were the eternal God.* (Psalm 90:1–2).

God is Almighty—*When Abram was ninety-nine years old, the*

LORD *appeared to him and said, "I am the Sovereign God. Walk before me and be blameless."* (Genesis 17:1).

God is Changeless— *"Since, I, the* LORD, *do not go back on my promises, you, sons of Jacob, have not perished.* (Malachi 3:6).

God is Omnipresent— *"Do you people think that I am some local deity and not the transcendent God?" the* LORD *asks. "Do you really think anyone can hide himself where I cannot see him?" the* LORD *asks. "Don't you know that I am everywhere?" the* LORD *asks.* (Jeremiah 23:23–24). *Where can I go to escape your spirit? Where can I flee to escape your presence? If I were to ascend to heaven, you would be there. If I were to sprawl out in Sheol, there you would be. If I were to fly away on the wings of the dawn, and settle down on the other side of the sea, even there your hand would guide me, your right hand would grab hold of me. If I were to say, "Certainly the darkness will cover me, and the light will turn to night all around me," even the darkness is not too dark for you to see, and the night is as bright as day; darkness and light are the same to you.* (Psalm 139:7–12).

God is Holy—*They called out to one another, "Holy, holy, holy is the* LORD *who leads armies! His majestic splendor fills the entire earth!"* (Isaiah 6:3).

God is Love—*In a far-off land the* LORD *will manifest himself to them. He will say to them, "I have loved you with an everlasting love. That is why I have continued to be faithful to you."* (Jeremiah 31:3).

God is Merciful—*And the* LORD *passed by before him and proclaimed: "The* LORD, *the* LORD, *the compassionate and gracious God, slow to anger, and abounding in loyal love and faithfulness, keeping loyal love for thousands, forgiving iniquity, and transgression and sin. But he by no means leaves the guilty unpunished, visiting the iniquity of the fathers on the children and on the children's children, to the third and fourth generation."* (Exodus 34:6–7).

God is Just— *Far be it from you to do such a thing—to kill the godly with the wicked, treating the godly and the wicked alike! Far be it from you! Will not the judge of the whole earth do what is right?* (Genesis 18:25).

This list merely introduces the vast subject of the nature of God. It is only by regularly and systematically reading the Bible that we really learn the greatness and majesty of God. Read carefully the following quotations. They reach great heights of poetic beauty as they describe the greatness and glory of God:

Do you not know? Have you not heard? The LORD is an eternal God, the creator of the whole earth. He does not get tired or weary; there is no limit to his wisdom. (Isaiah 40:28).

This is what the true God, the LORD, says—the one who created the sky and stretched it out, the one who fashioned the earth and everything that lives on it, the one who gives breath to the people on it, and life to those who live on it: "I, the LORD, officially commission you; I take hold of your hand. I protect you and make you a covenant mediator for people, and a light to the nations, to open blind eyes, to release prisoners from dungeons, those who live in darkness from prisons. I am the LORD! That is my name! I will not share my glory with anyone else, or the praise due me with idols." (Isaiah 42:5–8).

For this is what the LORD says, the one who created the sky—he is the true God, the one who formed the earth and made it; he established it, he did not create it without order, he formed it to be inhabited— "I am the LORD, I have no peer. I have not spoken in secret, in some hidden place. I did not tell Jacob's descendants, 'Seek me in vain.' I am the LORD, the one who speaks honestly, who makes reliable announcements. Gather together and come! Approach together, you refugees from the nations! Those who carry wooden idols know nothing, those who pray to a god that cannot deliver. Tell me! Present the evidence! Let them consult with one another! Who predicted this in the past? Who announced it beforehand? Was it not I, the LORD? I have no peer, there is no God but me, a God who vindicates and delivers; there is none but me. Turn to me so you can be delivered, all you who live in the earth's remote regions! For I am God, and I have no peer. I solemnly make this oath—what I say is true and reliable: 'Surely every knee will bow to me, every tongue will solemnly affirm'" (Isaiah 45:18–23).

These spiritual concepts were written by the prophet Isaiah about 2,500 years ago. Obviously there was nothing primitive or defective in the knowledge of God Isaiah and the other prophets brought to men.

4. GOD AS A GOD OF LOVE

Many people have misunderstood what is meant by the fact that God is a God of love. Because He is love, many have thought that God is indulgent of human sin, that He does not care whether or not men break His laws. God **is** love, but He is also absolutely holy and sin is an insult to Him and an outrage against His nature. Some have imagined that God's love and mercy are contradictory to and incompatible with His holiness and justice. This is not so. God in His justice and holiness cannot treat sinners indulgently. Sin must be punished unless it is forgiven in a way which is fully consistent with both the justice and the mercy of God. This is the message of the gospel! God has revealed a way in which a sinner can be forgiven and cleansed from his sin and thus enjoy the love and grace of God. Holiness, as an attribute of God, is not abstract purity-merely the absence of evil. It is a positive quality which reaches out to mankind. **God is love,** and therefore He does not want to punish sinners, and **God is holy,** and therefore He desires to restore sinners to a state of holiness and purity, fit for His eternal presence. The gospel tells us that God truly loves sinful people and has provided a salvation which transforms men and women into "sons of God," thus enabling them to share His eternal glory. Study this quotation from Romans 8:29–30:

> *Those whom he foreknew he also predestined to be conformed to the image of his Son, that his Son would be the firstborn among many brothers and sisters. And those he predestined, he also called; and those he called, he also justified; and those he justified, he also glorified.*

This revelation of the character and attributes of God is found in the Bible and nowhere else! As you continue your studies you will, we trust, come into this glorious fellowship with the God who, though so great in power and majesty, desires to save the weakest and worst sinners and make them His worshippers.

THE GOD OF THE BIBLE AND ALLAH OF THE QURAN

The following chart shows how God is revealed in the Bible and how Allah is spoken of in the Quran.

HEBREW TITLES OF GOD IN THE OLD TESTAMENT		
General	**Descriptive**	**Specific**
Elohim or God	Adonai or Lord=Master	Jehovah or LORD
This is used 2550 times	used 340 times	used 6823 times
ARABIC TITLES OF GOD USED IN THE QURAN		
Allah or God	Rabb or Lord=Master	No equivalent

One difference is quite evident. **Elohim** is approximately equivalent in meaning to **Allah. Adonai** is approximately equivalent in meaning to **Rabb,** but it can be seen that there is no Quranic equivalent for **Jehovah** (Y-H-W-H). The **Elohim-Allah** title describes God as the Almighty Creator. The **Adonai-Rabb** title describes God as Lord and Master over all His creatures. But it is in the Bible alone that we find God revealed as **Jehovah,** a title which is used over 6,800 times and which is the main name of God in the Bible. We all know names of God to be important because they reveal His character. Jehovah, as a Divine Name, is used in the Bible to depict God as the One who is Self-existing, and Self-revealing. As the Self-revealing God He reveals Himself as a God of grace who acts in redeeming love to rescue sinful men and women and restore them to fellowship and intimacy with Himself. Jehovah wants people to know Him and love Him while on earth, and then go to live with Him and share His glory for ever.

Jehovah in the Bible, as much as Allah in the Quran, is the Almighty Creator and Master. But He is also the God of redemption, love and grace, who says that, not only **may** we know Him in an intimate fellowship, but that all blessedness begins **when** we come to know Him. Read the following verses which emphasize the fact that God desires that man may know Him and enjoy His fellowship now and forever:

The LORD says, "Wise people should not boast that they are wise. Powerful people should not boast that they are powerful. Rich people should not boast that they are rich. If people want to boast, they should boast about this: They should boast that they understand and know me. They should boast that they know and understand that I, the LORD, act out of faithfulness, fairness, and justice in the earth and that I desire people to do these things," says the LORD. (Jeremiah 9:23–24).

I will give them the desire to acknowledge that I am the LORD. I will be their God and they will be my people. That is because they will wholeheartedly return to me.' (Jeremiah 24:7).

"People will no longer need to teach their neighbors and relatives to know me. That is because all of them, from the least important to the most important, will know me," says the LORD. "All of this is based on the fact that I will forgive their sin and will no longer call to mind the wrong they have done." (Jeremiah 31:34).

Now this is eternal life—that they know you, the only true God, and Jesus Christ, whom you sent. (John 17:3).

The concept which it is the essential purpose of the Bible to reveal is that God is **Jehovah,** the Redeemer who desires that men may know and love Him as a personal God.

CHAPTER THREE

⠿

WHAT IS A PROPHET?

In chapter one we made frequent references to the holy prophets. This raised a very important question; "What do we mean when we speak of prophets, and who are prophets?" We must find what the Bible says about this subject.

The first person in the Bible to be called a prophet was Abraham, the "Father of the Faithful." It is important to notice also, that it was God who gave him this title. The story is found in Genesis 20:6–7. A heathen prince had taken Abraham's wife, and God commanded him to restore her, saying of Abraham, "he is a prophet. . . ." (the Hebrew word is "nabi" as it is also in Arabic). Without doubt there were other men before Abraham who were prophets. Enoch was one, for instance (compare Genesis 5:24 with Jude 14). But Abraham was the first person to be designated a prophet by the clear Word of God. Many God-appointed prophets arose after Abraham. They were chosen from many walks of life. Moses was adopted in infancy by an Egyptian princess and thus received a prince's education. (Read in your Bible, for example, Exodus 2:5–10; Acts 7:21–22.) Ezekiel and Jeremiah were priests as well as prophets. David was first a shepherd, then warrior, king and poet and a prophet as well. Amos was a herdsman (Amos 1:1). Elisha was a plowman (1 Kings 19:15–21). Daniel was a government administrator (Daniel 2:48). From such diverse backgrounds, God chose His prophets. Their influence and authority did not come from their rank, education, wisdom or wealth, but entirely from the fact that God chose them to be His messengers. So we may define a prophet as one appointed by God Himself to be His messenger. Now we must examine the Bible to expand this brief definition. Notice first that God chose His messengers. The following Scriptures demonstrate this:

Now the LORD said to Abram, "Go out from your country, your relatives, and your father's household to the land that I will show you. Then I will make you into a great nation, and I will bless you, and I will make your name great, so that you will exemplify divine blessing. I will bless those who bless you, but the one who treats you lightly I must curse, and all the families of the earth will bless one another by your name." So Abram left, just as the LORD had told him to do, and Lot went with him. (Now Abram was seventy-five years old when he departed from Haran.) (Genesis 12:1–4).

Now Moses was shepherding the flock of Jethro his father-in-law, the priest of Midian, and he led the flock to the far side of the desert and came to the mountain of God, to Horeb. The Angel of the LORD appeared to him in a flame of fire from within a bush. He looked—and the bush was ablaze with fire, but it was not being consumed! So Moses thought, "I will turn aside to see this amazing sight. Why does the bush not burn up?" When the LORD saw that he had turned aside to look, God called to him from within the bush and said, "Moses, Moses!" And Moses said, "Here I am." God said, "Do not come near here. Take your sandals off your feet, for the place on which you are standing is holy ground." He also said, "I am the God of your father, the God of Abraham, the God of Isaac, and the God of Jacob." Then Moses hid his face, because he was afraid to look at God. The LORD said, "I have surely seen the affliction of my people who are in Egypt. I have heard their cry because of their taskmasters, for I know their sorrows. I have come down to deliver them from the hand of the Egyptians and to bring them up from that land to a land that is both good and large, to a land flowing with milk and honey, to the region of the Canaanites, Hittites, Amorites, Perizzites, Hivites, and Jebusites. And now, indeed, the cry of the Israelites has come to me, and I have also seen how severely the Egyptians oppress them. So now, go, and I will send you to Pharaoh to bring my people, the Israelites, out of Egypt." Moses said to God, "Who am I, that I should go to Pharaoh, or that I should bring the Israelites out of Egypt?" He replied, "Surely I will be with you, and this will be the sign to you that I have sent you: When you bring the people out of Egypt, you and they will serve God on this mountain." (Exodus 3:1–12).

Then the LORD came and stood nearby, calling as he had previously done, "Samuel! Samuel!" Samuel replied, "Speak, for your servant is listening!" The LORD said to Samuel, "Look! I am about to do something in Israel; when anyone hears about it, both of his ears will tingle." (1 Samuel 3:10–11).

The LORD said to me, "Before I formed you in your mother's womb I chose you. Before you were born I set you apart. I appointed you to be a prophet to the nations." I answered, "Oh, Lord GOD, I really do not know how to speak well enough for that, for I am too young. The LORD said to me, "Do not say, 'I am too young.' But go to whomever I send you and say whatever I tell you. Do not be afraid of those to whom I send you, for I will be with you to rescue you," says the LORD. Then the LORD reached out his hand and touched my mouth and said to me, "I will most assuredly give you the words you are to speak for me. Know for certain that I hereby give you the authority to announce to nations and kingdoms that they will be uprooted and torn down, destroyed and demolished, rebuilt and firmly planted." (Jeremiah 1:5–10).

God in His wisdom chose men who would obey Him faithfully and He gave them authority to speak on His behalf. Prophets were not chosen or elected by men, and they were not permitted to inherit the title or regard it as an official post to be filled by a man specially trained for it.

Notice also that **God told them what to do.** We may find example of the work of a true prophet in a number of references as follows. Their work was:

1. TO REVEAL THE NATURE AND ATTRIBUTES OF GOD TO MEN.

The following Scriptures show this:

The LORD spoke face to face with you at the mountain, from the middle of the fire. (I was standing between the LORD and you then to reveal to you the message of the LORD, because you were afraid of the fire and would not go up the mountain.) He said: "I am the LORD your God, he who brought you from the land of Egypt, from the place of slavery. You must not have any other gods besides me. You must not make for yourself an image of anything in heaven above, on earth below, or in the waters beneath. You must not worship or serve them, for I, the LORD your God, am a jealous God. I punish the sons, grandsons, and great-grandsons for the sin of the fathers who reject me, but I show covenant faithfulness to the thousands who choose me and keep my commandments." (Deuteronomy 5:4–10).

The LORD spoke to Moses: "Speak to the whole congregation of the Israelites and tell them, 'You must be holy because I, the LORD your God, am holy. Each of you must respect his mother and his father, and you must keep my Sabbaths. I am the LORD your God. Do not turn to idols, and you must not make for yourselves gods of cast metal. I am the LORD your God.'" (Leviticus 19:1–4).

2. *TO MAKE KNOWN TO MEN THE LAWS OF GOD.*

For example Exodus 20:1–17 says:

And God spoke all these words: "I, the LORD, am your God, who brought you from the land of Egypt, from the house of bondage. You shall have no other gods before me. You shall not make for yourself a carved image or any likeness of anything that is in heaven above, or that is on earth under it, or that is in the water below. You shall not bow down to them or serve them, for I, the LORD, your God, am a jealous God, who visits the iniquity of fathers on children, even to the third and fourth generations of those who hate me, but who extends faithful love to a thousand generations of those who love me and keep my commandments. You shall not take the name of the LORD your God in vain, for the LORD will not hold guiltless anyone who takes his name in vain. Remember the Sabbath day to sanctify it. For six days you may labor and do all your work, but the seventh day is a Sabbath to the LORD your God; on it you shall not do any work, you, or your son, or your daughter, or your male servant, or your female servant, or your cattle, or your resident foreigner who is in your gates. For in six days the LORD made the heavens and the earth and the sea and all that is in them, and he rested on the seventh day; therefore the LORD blessed the Sabbath day and sanctified it. Honor your father and your mother, that your days may be long in the land the LORD your God is giving to you. You shall not murder. You shall not commit adultery. You shall not steal. You shall not give false testimony against your neighbor. You shall not covet your neighbor's house. You shall not covet your neighbor's wife, nor his male servant, nor his female servant, nor his ox, nor his donkey, nor anything that belongs to your neighbor."

3. *To call the people back to obedience to God's laws.*

Read 2 Chronicles 24:19— *The LORD sent prophets among them to lead them back to him. They warned the people, but they would not pay attention.*

4. *To exhort the people to sincerity in worship.*

An example of this is found in Jeremiah 7:1–11:

The LORD said to Jeremiah: "Stand in the gate of the LORD's temple and proclaim this message: 'Listen, all you people of Judah who have passed through these gates to worship the LORD. Hear what the LORD has to say. The LORD God of Israel who rules over all says: Change the way you have been living and do what is right. If you do, I will let you continue to live in this land. Stop putting your confidence in the delusive belief that says, "We are safe! The temple of the LORD is here! The temple of the LORD is here! The temple of the LORD is here!" You must change the way you have been living and do what is right. You must treat one another fairly. Stop oppressing foreigners who live in your land, children who have lost their fathers, and women who have lost their husbands. Stop killing innocent people in this land. Stop paying allegiance to other gods. That will only bring about your ruin. If you do all this, I will let you continue to live here in this land which I gave to your ancestors as a lasting possession.

"But just look at you! You are putting your confidence in a false way of thinking that will not help you at all. You steal. You murder. You commit adultery. You lie when you swear on oath. You sacrifice to the god Baal. You pay allegiance to other gods that you do not really know. Then you come and stand here in my presence in this house I have claimed as my own and say, "We are safe!" You think you are so safe that you go on doing all those hateful sins! Do you think this house I have claimed as my own is to be a hideout for robbers? You had better take note! I have seen for myself what you have done! says the LORD."'

5. *TO WARN THEM OF DIVINE JUDGMENT UPON SIN, BOTH PERSONAL AND NATIONAL.*

See Jeremiah 36:30–31:

So the LORD says concerning King Jehoiakim of Judah, "None of his line will occupy the throne of David. And his dead body will be thrown out to be exposed to scorching heat by day and frost by night. I will punish him and his descendants and the officials who serve him for the wicked things they have done. I will bring on them and the citizens of Jerusalem and the people of Judah all the disaster that I threatened to do to them. I will punish them because I threatened them but they still paid no heed."

6. *TO FORETELL FUTURE EVENTS WHICH GOD HAD WILLED.*

A good illustration of this would be Jeremiah 30:1–3:

The LORD spoke to Jeremiah. He said, "The LORD God of Israel who rules over all says, 'Write everything that I am about to tell you in a scroll. For I, the LORD affirm that the time will come when I will reverse the fortunes of my people, Israel and Judah,' says the LORD. 'I will bring them back to the land I gave their ancestors and they will take possession of it once again.'"

7. *TO FORETELL THE COMING OF THE MESSIAH, THE SAVIOR.*

See for example Isaiah 9:6:

For a child has been born to us, a son has been given to us. He shoulders responsibility and is called: Extraordinary Strategist, Mighty God, Everlasting Father, Prince of Peace.

8. TO RECORD THE HISTORY OF GOD'S DEALINGS WITH MEN.

An example of this is in Deuteronomy 31:9–13:

Then Moses wrote down this law and gave it to the Levitical priests, who carry the ark of the LORD's covenant, and to all Israel's elders. He commanded them: "At the end of seven years, at the appointed time of the cancellation of debts, at the Feast of Temporary Shelters, when all Israel comes to appear before the LORD your God in the place he chooses, you must read this law before them within their hearing. Gather the people—men, women, and children, as well as the resident foreigners in your villages—so they may hear and thus learn about and fear the LORD your God and carefully obey all the words of this law. Then their children, who have not known this law, will also hear about and learn to fear the LORD your God for as long as you live in the land you are crossing the Jordan to possess."

9. TO RECORD THE WORD OF GOD IN THE HOLY SCRIPTURES.

The following are examples of this:

And the LORD said to Moses, "Write this as a memorial in the book, and rehearse it in Joshua's hearing; for I will surely wipe out the remembrance of Amalek from under the heavens." (Exodus 17:14).

And the LORD said to Moses, "Write these words, for in accordance with these words I have made a covenant with you and with Israel." (Exodus 34:27).

So on that day Moses wrote down this song and taught it to the Israelites, and the LORD commissioned Joshua son of Nun, "Be strong and courageous, for you will take the Israelites to the land I have promised them, and I will be with you." When Moses finished writing on a scroll the words of this law in their entirety, he commanded the Levites who carried the ark of the LORD's covenant, "Take this scroll of the law and place it beside the ark of the covenant of the LORD *your God. It will remain there as a witness against you"* (Deuteronomy 31:22–26).

The LORD *spoke to Jeremiah in the fourth year that Jehoiakim son of Josiah was ruling over Judah. He said, "Get a scroll. Write on it everything I have told you to say about Israel, Judah, and all the other nations since I began to speak to you in the reign of Josiah until now.* (Jeremiah 36:1–2).

The LORD *spoke to Jeremiah after Jehoiakim had burned the scroll containing what Jeremiah had spoken and Baruch had written down. He said, "Get another scroll and write on it everything that was written on the original scroll that King Jehoiakim of Judah burned."* (Jeremiah 36:27–28).

This list is by no means complete but it shows the importance of the work of a prophet. Even the humblest and most ordinary men became important, influential and authoritative in Israel when called to be prophets. Some prophets were called to challenge the whole nation (1 Kings 18:21), or to rebuke evil kings (1 Kings 21:17–24; Daniel 5:17–28) and many were given power to perform miracles to support their authority. An example of this is in Exodus 17:5–6 *And the* LORD *said to Moses, "Go over before the people; take with you some of the elders of Israel and take in your hand your rod with which you struck the Nile and go. I will be standing before you there on the rock in Horeb, and you will strike the rock, and water will come out of it so that the people may drink." And Moses did so in plain view of the elders of Israel.* In the nation of Israel, prophets were more important than kings, warriors or priests.

Because the prophets were so influential, it is not surprising that early in history, false prophets appeared, pretending to be God's messengers in order to support their own ambitions for power, authority and personal advancement. Because of this, God gave clear instructions to the people to examine the credentials of all who claimed to be prophets. These Divine instructions are found in Deuteronomy 18:9–22. This paragraph is so important that the student should read it before going any further with this lesson. Here it is:

> *When you enter the land the LORD your God is giving you, you must not learn the abhorrent practices of those nations. There must never be found among you anyone who sacrifices his son or daughter in the fire, anyone who practices divination, an omen reader, a soothsayer, a sorcerer, one who casts spells, one who conjures up spirits, a practitioner of the occult, or a necromancer. Whoever does these things is abhorrent to the LORD and because of these things the LORD your God is about to drive them out from before you. You must be blameless before the LORD your God. Those nations that you are about to dispossess listen to omen readers and diviners, but the LORD your God has not given you permission to do such things. The LORD your God will raise up for you a prophet like me from among you—from your fellow Israelites; you must listen to him. This accords with what happened at Horeb in the day of the assembly. You asked the LORD your God: "Please do not make us hear the voice of the LORD our God any more or see this great fire any more lest we die." The LORD then said to me, "What they have said is good. I will raise up a prophet like you for them from among their fellow Israelites. I will put my words in his mouth and he will speak to them whatever I command. I will personally hold responsible anyone who then pays no attention to the words that prophet speaks in my name. "But if any prophet presumes to speak anything in my name that I have not authorized him to speak, or speaks in the name of other gods, that prophet must die. Now if you say to yourselves, 'How can we tell that a message is not from the LORD?'—whenever a prophet speaks in my name and the prediction is not fulfilled, then I have not spoken it; the prophet has presumed to speak it, so you need not fear him."*

Notice that God warned the people that all pagan practices and customs were strictly forbidden. In particular, God warned them not to seek help or guidance through occult practices like divination, witchcraft or necromancy (the belief that spirits of dead people can be used to obtain help). We are expressly told, *Whoever does these things is abhorrent to the* LORD. As these practices were strictly forbidden, how were the people of Israel to obtain help and guidance? God gave them a clear answer; *I will raise up for you a prophet like me from among you. . . .* God would not permit pagan methods of seeking help, but He would appoint His own prophets through whom He would speak and guide those who desired to know the truth. From this important Scripture we find certain definite rules by which the people could know a true prophet sent by God.

A TRUE PROPHET SPEAKS IN THE NAME OF JEHOVAH

We have already explained that this name of God, used so frequently in the Bible, was spelled by the Hebrew consonants Y.H.W.H. and was probably pronounced Yahweh, but is found in our English Bibles either as Jehovah or more often as LORD. In the passage just quoted we find 10 occurrences of this Divine title. God, speaking through Moses, made it clear that only those prophets who spoke in the name of Jehovah were to be accepted.

A TRUE PROPHET WILL BE CHOSEN BY GOD FROM ONE OF THE TRIBES OF ISRAEL

Verse 18 says he shall be *from among their fellow Israelites.* Moses was speaking to Israelites and it is clear that he said that God would raise up a prophet *from among you* (verse 15). This same expression (*fellow Israelites*) is found in Deuteronomy 3:18 and Deuteronomy 17:15 where God said that the future kings of Israel must be chosen from among their brethren—they were not to set a foreigner over them as their king. Thus it is clear the prophet must be an Israelite.

A TRUE PROPHET WILL SPEAK THE WORDS WHICH JEHOVAH PUTS INTO HIS MOUTH

God's message is often rejected by sinful men because God demands obedience to His Word, but a true prophet will not try to make his message popular. A false prophet however appeals to popular enthusiasm.

Notice the example in Isaiah 30:8–11 where the people ask the false prophets to prophesy nice things—*Now go, write it down on a tablet in their presence, inscribe it on a scroll, so that it might be saved for a future time as an enduring witness. For these are rebellious people—they are lying children, children unwilling to obey the LORD's law. They say to the visionaries, "See no more visions!" and to the seers, "Don't relate messages to us about what is right! Tell us nice things, relate deceptive messages. Turn aside from the way, stray off the path. Remove from our presence the sovereign king of Israel."* Jeremiah shows us that a true prophet does not invent his message—he is inspired by God— *Then the LORD reached out his hand and touched my mouth and said to me, "I will most assuredly give you the words you are to speak for me."* (Jeremiah 1:9).

A TRUE PROPHET WILL BE VINDICATED BY THE FULFILLMENT OF HIS MESSAGE

Again Jeremiah gives a clear illustration of this. Read Jeremiah 14:14–16:

Then the LORD said to me, "Those prophets are prophesying lies while claiming my authority. I did not send them. I did not commission them. And I did not speak to them. They are just prophesying to these people false visions, worthless predictions, and the delusions of their own mind. I did not send those prophets, though they claim to be prophesying in my authority. They may be saying, 'No war or famine will happen in this land.' But I, the LORD, say this about them: 'War and starvation will kill those prophets.' And the people to whom they are prophesying will die through war and famine. Their bodies will be thrown out into the streets of Jerusalem and they won't even be buried. That will happen to the men and their wives, their sons, and their daughters. For I will pour out on them the destruction they deserve."

God had told Jeremiah to announce that Jerusalem would be captured by the Babylonian army, as a punishment for the sins of the people. False prophets opposed Jeremiah and denied his words, suggesting that he was a traitor. But God said that the false prophets themselves would die by the sword of the Babylonians. This was literally fulfilled, and thus the words of Jeremiah were proved to be God's message, while the popular message of the false prophets was shown to be lies, even though they had dared to use the name of Jehovah. A similar incident is seen in 1 Kings 22:5–28 where Micaiah was sent to prison for speaking God's word, but the king who foolishly believed the words of the false prophets was killed in battle.

A FALSE PROPHET MUST BE PUT TO DEATH FOR TEACHING REBELLION AGAINST JEHOVAH, THE GOD OF THE ISRAELITES

This commandment is found in the following Scriptures:

Suppose a prophet or one who foretells by dreams should appear among you and show you a sign or wonder, and the sign or wonder should come to pass concerning what he said to you, namely, "Let us follow other gods"—gods whom you have not previously known—"and let us serve them." You must not listen to the words of that prophet or dreamer, for the LORD your God will be testing you to see if you love him with all your mind and being. You must follow the LORD your God and revere only him; and you must observe his commandments, obey him, serve him, and remain loyal to him. As for that prophet or dreamer, he must be executed because he encouraged rebellion against the LORD your God who brought you from the land of Egypt, redeeming you from the place of slavery, and because he has tried to entice you from the way the LORD your God has commanded you to go. In this way you must purge out evil from within (Deuteronomy 13:1–5)

But if any prophet presumes to speak anything in my name that I have not authorized him to speak, or speaks in the name of other gods, that prophet must die (Deuteronomy 18:20)

The severity of this penalty emphasizes how dangerous false prophets are. No matter how important a person might be, or however closely he might be related to the king or anyone who might help decide his fate, he was to be treated as a traitor if he dared to speak a message that turned people away from the worship of Jehovah.

In all these verses notice the constant emphasis on the words, *the LORD (Jehovah) your God.* Pagan nations had degraded the meaning of the word God (Elohim) to include their idols, and so God the Creator stated that henceforth He would be known by His personal name, Jehovah. Not only was this a distinguishing feature of the worship of the One True God, but we find that the oft–repeated expression *the name of the LORD* was a Hebrew idiom which means "**in the authority of the LORD**" and "**in the character of the LORD.**" Thus a prophet who spoke in the name of Jehovah was speaking by the authority of Jehovah and in the character of Jehovah. Jehovah is holy, therefore the message must be holy in character and the messenger must likewise display the holiness of life which would be evidence of his truthfulness.

All prophets were to be tested thus concerning the origin of their words, and the meaning and the purpose of their teaching. That teaching must come from Jehovah; it must be true to the earlier revelation of the character of Jehovah, and it must be designed to encourage men to be faithful to Jehovah. Put these points together and you will find God's method for testing the credentials of a true prophet:

1. He must be a true Israelite.
2. He must speak in the name of the LORD (Jehovah).
3. He must call men to living obedience to Jehovah and worship of Jehovah.
4. He must be tested and vindicated by the fulfillment of predictions made by him in the name of Jehovah, by the authority of Jehovah and in keeping with the character of Jehovah.

This explains why the prophets of the Old Testament and the apostles in the New Testament were members of the Hebrew (Israelite) people. Apart from these Biblical prophets and apostles, no man has ever been known to fulfill the Divine requirements laid down in the above verses. Many men have claimed to be leaders, teachers and prophets, but when we examine their credentials, we find that they were not members of the Hebrew race, nor did they speak in the name of Jehovah.

Thus the Bible alone contains the authentic teachings of God's chosen messengers, prophets and apostles, and although the message of the Bible is not a popular one that appeals to the hearts of proud men, it is the Word of God and shows the way to eternal life.

There is one final comment which is of vital importance to this study. We have noted that God revealed the criteria for the recognition of a true prophet. But the verses in Deuteronomy 18 go further than that. They contain a definite prediction of the coming of a specific prophet. The Jews always understood this verse to be a clear promise concerning the coming Messiah. This is clear from the following verses. Read for example John 1:19–23 and note that when John the Baptist began to preach, he was asked, *"Are you the Prophet?"* Now *this was John's testimony when the Jewish leaders sent priests and Levites from Jerusalem to ask him, "Who are you?" He confessed—he did not deny but confessed—"I am not the Christ!" So they asked him, "Then who are you? Are you Elijah?" He said, "I am not!" "Are you the Prophet?" He answered, "No!" Then they said to him, "Who are you? Tell us so that we can give an answer to those who sent us. What do you say about yourself?" John said, "I am the voice of one shouting in the wilderness, 'Make straight the way for the Lord,' as Isaiah the prophet said."* Also in John 6:14 we see how the people, impressed by the power of Jesus, said, *Now when the people saw the miraculous sign that Jesus performed, they began to say to one another, "This is certainly the Prophet who is to come into the world."* In John 7:40 again the people said, *When they heard these words, some of the crowd began to say, "This really is the Prophet!"* It is clear that the Jewish people expected a precise and personal fulfillment of this prophecy and when John the Baptist appeared they thought he was **The** Prophet, but John humbly disclaimed that honor, and directed their attention to Jesus—*(Now they had been sent from the Pharisees.) So they asked John, "Why then are you baptizing if you are not the Christ, nor Elijah, nor the Prophet?" John answered them, "I baptize with water. Among you stands one whom you do not recognize, who is coming after me. I am not worthy to untie the strap of his sandal!" These things happened in Bethany across the Jordan River where John* *was baptizing. On the next day John saw Jesus coming toward him and said, "Look, the Lamb of God who takes away the sin of the world! This is the one about whom I said, 'After me comes a man who is greater than I am, because he existed before me.'"* (John 1:24–30). The people then recognized Jesus as the Prophet. The people were right in thus recognizing Jesus as The Prophet. The Apostle Peter clearly taught that the great prediction was completely fulfilled in Jesus Christ. We read:

> *Therefore repent and turn back so that your sins may be wiped out, so that times of refreshing may come from the presence of the Lord, and so that he may send the Messiah appointed for you—that is, Jesus. This one heaven must receive until the time all things are restored, which God declared from times long ago through his holy prophets. Moses said, "The Lord your God will raise up for you a prophet like me from among your brothers. You must obey him in everything he tells you. Every person who does not obey that prophet will be destroyed and thus removed from the people" And all the prophets, from Samuel and those who followed him, have spoken about and announced these days You are the sons of the prophets and of the covenant that God made with your ancestors, saying to Abraham, "And in your descendants all the nations of the earth will be blessed.' God raised up his servant and sent him first to you, to bless you by turning each one of you from your iniquities."* (Acts 3:19–26).

This one short paragraph then in Deuteronomy 18 contains remarkable truth. It sets out for all time the criteria for the recognition of a true prophet, and also a prediction of the coming of The True Prophet, a prediction which was finally and perfectly fulfilled in the coming of Jesus Christ. When Jesus came to the Jews, He fulfilled all the conditions of the prediction in Deuteronomy and thus His disciples accepted Him as the promised Prophet and Messiah. So certain is this fact that the Apostle Peter said, *Every person who does not obey that prophet will be destroyed and thus removed from the people.'* (Acts 3:23). This is a solemn warning to those who reject the claims of Jesus Christ.

CHAPTER FOUR

THE CONTINUITY OF DOCTRINE

A study of the authority of the Bible sooner or later means facing a problem which has confused many people, and which presents particular difficulties to Jews and Muslims. It is a double question (1) What do Christians mean by the terms "The Old Testament" and "The New Testament"? (2) What relationship exists between the Hebrew Old Testament and the Christian New Testament? This problem is heightened by the fact that the Jews do not accept the New Testament while Muslims accept both, in theory.

THE BIBLE IS ONE COMPLETE BOOK

The Bible is one complete Book consisting of Old and New Testaments. In other words, there is direct continuity of Divine revelation and authority running right through all sixty-six books of the Bible. No one part contradicts another part, and if one part were to be missing there would be an obvious gap in the whole Book. There is not the slightest hint in the Bible that the earlier revelations were to be contradicted or cancelled by the New Testament. The casual reader might possibly find **apparent** contradictions. Serious study however makes it clear that the later parts of the Bible are not contradictory but complementary. They are given as a further development of the earlier revelation in order to give a wider understanding of an important subject. For instance, when a child commences school, he learns the basic use of the alphabet and numerals. For the rest of his school life he learns additional facts about the use of letters and numbers until he is acquainted with extensive literature and able to handle advanced mathematics. The things he learns later do not ever contradict his beginning lessons; they simply add to his original inadequate understanding. This was the method chosen by an all-wise God in revealing Himself to mankind.

Now note the theme of the following quotations. Isaiah says, *The decree of our God is forever reliable* (Isaiah 40:6–8). Matthew says, *I tell you the truth, until heaven and earth pass away not the smallest letter or stroke of a letter will pass from the law until everything takes place* (Matthew 5:18). Peter says, *but the word of the Lord endures forever* (1 Peter 1:25). These three verses plainly state that God's Word will never pass away. Note that one quotation is from an Old Testament prophet, one is from the teaching of Jesus Christ and one is from the teaching of the Apostle Peter. This shows that any theory of abrogation is unfounded; on the contrary, the Bible is the record of a continuous, coherent, developing revelation which will never pass away.

THE OLD TESTAMENT IS THE FOUNDATION OF ALL DIVINE REVELATION

Logically, the Bible begins at the very beginning! *In the beginning God created the heavens and the earth* (Genesis 1:1). *God created mankind in his own image, in the image of God he created them, male and female he created them* (Genesis 1:27). All ancient nations have stories of a "beginning" but most of those stories are an absurd mixture of myth and legend and are not worth even considering as a Divine revelation. The book of Genesis is remarkably simple in its narrative and yet it contains the beginnings of all the major themes developed and expanded throughout the rest of the Bible. Note some of these major topics.

1. THE BEGINNING OF THE UNIVERSE

The universe did not come into existence by chance but by the will and power of God. He created the earth to be a home for mankind. Science has so far discovered no other planet which has the right conditions for human life. Our earth is unique.

2. THE BEGINNINGS OF THE HUMAN RACE

Why did God create man? No one will know the complete answer to that question in this life, but God has given some interesting clues concerning His purpose. Man was created to be God's "viceroy" to govern the earth for Him (Genesis 1:26). This helps explain why people aspire to positions of authority, and why they have such an urge to investigate and tabulate scientific facts about the universe and all it contains. God created man for this purpose and endowed the human race with the intelligence to study nature. The increase of knowledge and the growth of science are proofs of God's purpose in creating man. Man's search for knowledge has been accompanied, unfortunately, by pride with the result that clever men are apt to turn away from God. Because man rebelled against his Creator (Genesis 3), human authority has been tainted by injustice, cruelty, pride and abuse of power ever since.

Man was created with spiritual qualities which set him apart from the animals. No animal has the power of intelligent free choice. This power was given to man by God to enable us to willingly love, serve and worship our Creator. The Bible constantly emphasizes the truth that God desires intelligent worship from man. For example we read in John 4:23—*But a time is coming—and now is here—when the true worshipers will worship the Father in spirit and truth, for the Father seeks such people to be his worshipers.*

3. THE BEGINNING OF SIN IN HUMAN LIFE

Sin is a mystery, but we are told that, so far as the human race is concerned, it began with man's disobedience of God's laws. The Bible makes it plain that each person is responsible for his own sin. We **chose** to disobey.

4. THE BEGINNING OF GOD'S PLAN OF SALVATION FROM SIN

Though man sinned and rebelled, God still loves people and plans to save them. The initiative for our salvation comes from God. Other religions claim that man is seeking for God but the Bible teaches that God is seeking for men.

5. THE BEGINNING OF THE NATIONS

The story of the beginning of the nations is given in Genesis 11:1–9. Men are of different races and different cultures but all are part of the one human race and all are equally important in God's sight. Paul says:

From one man he made every nation of the human race to inhabit the entire earth, determining their set times and the fixed limits of the places where they would live, so that they would search for God and perhaps grope around for him and find him, though he is not far from each one of us. For in him we live and move about and exist, as even some of your own poets have said, "For we too are his offspring" (Acts 17:26–28).

6. THE BEGINNING OF THE HEBREW PEOPLE

The call of Abraham gave the first clear indication of the way God would fulfill His plan for the salvation of mankind. We shall see more of this in later lessons.

7. THE BEGINNING OF FAITH IN HUMAN LIFE

From the beginning, God blessed those who trusted and obeyed Him. This is the principle through the entire Bible. *Now without faith it is impossible to please him, for the one who approaches God must believe that he exists and that he rewards those who seek him* (Hebrews 11:6).

8. THE BEGINNING OF GOD'S REVELATION OF HIMSELF TO MEN

Genesis does not give a final and complete revelation of God, but the basic facts are given as a foundation on which later revelations are built.

THE OLD TESTAMENT CONTAINS A RECORD OF GOD'S LOVE AND GRACE

Although mankind sinned against God, He continued to reveal His love to men. This is shown first in the stories of men of faith like Abraham, Isaac, Jacob and Joseph. Later the story is expanded to show God's love for the people of Israel. For centuries God sent His prophets to the sinful and rebellious Israelites to warn them of the consequences of sin, and to promise them rich blessings if they would obey Him.

THE OLD TESTAMENT CONTAINS THE LAWS OF GOD FOR HUMAN LIFE

Moses is called the great Lawgiver, but he was not the first man to know God's laws. Long before Moses was even born God revealed His laws for human conduct to Adam, to Noah, to Abraham and to others, Moses, however, was entrusted by God with the task of teaching men the great written Code which includes the Ten Commandments. The laws of God were given to guide man in his worship, and in his moral, and social obligations.

THE OLD TESTAMENT CONTAINS THE PROMISES OF GOD CONCERNING THE COMING OF THE MESSIAH, THE SAVIOR

In a later chapter we will examine some of these promises in detail. We simply point out here that from the beginning of human history God promised a Savior for mankind. As the centuries rolled by, God gave hundreds of specific predictions concerning the coming Messiah. But this brings us to a very mysterious problem for the Hebrew Scriptures (the Old Testament) came to a complete and abrupt end with the book of Malachi at about 400 B.C. Yet the promise of God had not been fulfilled! Is God true? Why did He not fulfill His promises to the prophets and the waiting people?

There is only one answer to this problem. The promises in the Old Testament pointed forward to a future time. The time was known only to God, although as we shall see later, He planted certain "clues" in the Old Testament about even the time and the place at which He would fulfill His promises. The Old Testament then is obviously a book of beginnings, a book of Divine revelations and a book of Divine promises, but it does not record the fulfillment of the prophets' teaching. Where do we find that?—**in the New Testament!** The Old Testament is a foundation upon which something else is built. That something is the New Testament in which we have the completion of the Old Testament promises. Thus the Bible consists of these two important parts—the Old Testament being a record of Divine promises and the New Testament being a record of the way in which God fulfilled His promises. That this is not a mere theory anyone can find out for himself by diligently comparing the Old Testament with the New.

THE OLD TESTAMENT CONTAINS GOD'S PROMISE CONCERNING THE NEW TESTAMENT

This remarkable fact demonstrates the essential unity of the Bible. Jeremiah was one of the greatest of the Hebrew prophets, and he lived in the dramatic period which saw the collapse of the kingdom of Judah. In clear and plain words, God told the people through Jeremiah that **there would be a "New Testament."** Read carefully the following paragraph:

"Indeed, a time is coming," says the LORD, "when I will make a new agreement with the people of Israel and Judah. It will not be like the old agreement that I made with their ancestors when I took them by the hand and led them out of Egypt. For they violated that agreement, even though I was a faithful husband to them," says the LORD. "But I will make a new agreement with the whole nation of Israel after I plant them back in the land," says the LORD. "I will put my law within them and write it on their hearts and minds. And I will be their God and they will be my people. "People will no longer need to teach their neighbors and relatives to know me. That is because all of them, from the least important to the most important, will know me," says the LORD. "All of this is based on the fact that I will forgive their sin and will no longer call to mind the wrong they have done." (Jeremiah 31:31–34).

The New Covenant (Covenant, Testament and Agreement as used in the NET Bible Translation are synonymous English words) was given to bring in God's plan for the forgiveness of sin (verse 34). God clearly foretold the making of a new covenant (agreement) to fulfill the old one and stated in advance that the central feature of the New Testament was to be the forgiveness of sin. It is evident then that there is continuity of purpose through the entire Bible. It is of great personal importance to us to see that this purpose is centered in the promise of a Savior, who would take away sin and give people a new heart, one on which God would "write His laws" so that sinners can be restored to fellowship with God. Now comes a very personal question —Do you have the assurance that God has forgiven your sins? God has given us the Bible to reveal to us His love and grace for sinful men and women. He has recorded the promises of the coming Savior, and has told how the Savior came. The responsibility now rests with us to examine the facts and to find this way of salvation of which the Bible speaks.

CHAPTER FIVE

PROPHECIES CONCERNING CHRIST

THE ANOINTED ONE

There is so much written in the Bible about the Messiah that we obviously must be selective. We shall choose some of the main prophecies and predictions which relate to the coming of the promised Messiah, and show how they were fulfilled in precise detail in New Testament times. What does the word "Messiah" mean? It is a Hebrew word which really means the "anointed One." Right through the Old Testament period certain people were "anointed" with oil as a sign that God had chosen them for special tasks. Two kinds of appointment were made in this way. Priests were thus anointed. We read of Aaron, for example. *He then poured some of the anointing oil on the head of Aaron and anointed him to consecrate him.* (Leviticus 8:12). Kings were also anointed. Thus we read of David:

> *So Jesse had him brought in. Now he was ruddy, with attractive eyes and a handsome appearance. The LORD said, "Go and anoint him. This is the one!" So Samuel took the horn full of olive oil and anointed him in the midst of his brothers. The Spirit of the LORD rushed upon David from that day onwards. Then Samuel got up and went to Ramah.* (1 Samuel 16:12–13).

As time passed, the expression "the Messiah" took on the meaning of the "Chosen One" among the Hebrew people and it became a proper name for the Savior God had promised would come.

THE NEED FOR A SAVIOR

Why does the Bible contain promises about a coming Savior? The answer to this question becomes obvious as we examine the evidence, commencing with the very first promise in the Bible. This promise is found in Genesis 3 and the story connected with it is well known. It tells how Adam and Eve were tempted by Satan into disobeying God. Until then, no sin had come between God and man. Man's disobedience changed the perfect relationship which had existed between God and the human race for when man became sinful he feared the holiness of God. Here is the Biblical narrative: *But the LORD God called to the man and said to him, "Where are you?" The man replied, "I heard you moving about in the orchard, and I was afraid because I was naked, so I hid."* (Genesis 3:9–10).

Today, men are inclined to ridicule the idea that sin is serious, but that is a very foolish attitude. Proverbs 14:9 says: *Fools mock at reparation, but among the upright there is favor.* Because God is the Almighty Creator, anything affecting our relationship with Him is extremely serious. The Bible makes it clear that sin is the most serious thing in human life for it will separate us from God forever unless we can find the way of forgiveness of sin.

Because God is merciful, He does not leave us to try to discover the way to forgiveness by our own efforts. At the very moment Adam and Eve became aware of the fatal consequences of sin God gave the first promise of a coming Savior. Because Satan was the tempter, God said to him, *And I will put hostility between you and the woman and between your offspring and her offspring; her offspring will attack your head, and you will attack her offspring's heel.* (Genesis 3:15).

THE FIRST GREAT PROMISE

What does this strange promise mean? Certainly it was expressed in symbolic language, but nevertheless it contains some very clear points. It declares that there would be permanent enmity between Satan and the human race; that the power of Satan would eventually be overcome by a human being, and that in the process of destroying the power of Satan, the Savior would suffer. In crushing Satan's "head," the Savior's "heel" would be attacked. Moreover, the Savior would be "the offspring of the woman" This last statement is somewhat unusual. Why was the coming Savior not called the offspring of the man? Most races trace the lines of inheritance through the male. To answer this question we must leap over thousands of years and read what is written in the book of the prophet Isaiah. *For this reason the sovereign master [God] himself will give you a confirming sign. Look, this young woman [virgin] is about to conceive and will give birth to a son. You, young woman, will name him Immanuel.* (Isaiah 7:14). This prophecy has a direct connection with the subject but, as we showed in an earlier lesson, the final answer to questions in the Old Testament is found in the New Testament.

Now read the two passages which follow taken from the New Testament:

Now the birth of Jesus Christ happened this way. While his mother Mary was engaged to Joseph, but before they came together, she was found to be pregnant through the Holy Spirit. Because Joseph, her husband to be, was a righteous man, and because he did not want to disgrace her, he intended to divorce her privately. When he had contemplated this, an angel of the Lord appeared to him in a dream and said, "Joseph, son of David, do not be afraid to take Mary as your wife, because the child conceived in her is from the Holy Spirit. She will give birth to a son and you will name him Jesus, because he will save his people from their sins." This all happened so that what was spoken by the Lord through the prophet would be fulfilled: "Look! The virgin will conceive and bear a son, and they will call him Emmanuel," which means "God with us." When Joseph awoke from sleep he did what the angel of the Lord told him. He took his wife, but did not have marital relations with her until she gave birth to a son, whom he named Jesus (Matthew 1:18–25).

In the sixth month of Elizabeth's pregnancy, the angel Gabriel was sent by God to a town of Galilee called Nazareth, to a virgin engaged to a man whose name was Joseph, a descendant of David, and the virgin's name was Mary. The angel came to her and said, "Greetings, favored one, the Lord is with you!" But she was greatly troubled by his words and began to wonder about the meaning of this greeting. So the angel said to her, "Do not be afraid, Mary, for you have found favor with God! Listen: You will become pregnant and give birth to a son, and you will name him Jesus. He will be great, and will be called the Son of the Most High, and the Lord

God will give him the throne of his father David. He will reign over the house of Jacob forever, and his kingdom will never end." Mary said to the angel, "How will this be, since I have not had sexual relations with a man?" The angel replied, "The Holy Spirit will come upon you, and the power of the Most High will overshadow you. Therefore the child to be born will be holy; he will be called the Son of God. "And look, your relative Elizabeth has also become pregnant with a son in her old age—although she was called barren, she is now in her sixth month! For nothing will be impossible with God." So Mary said, "Yes, I am a servant of the Lord; let this happen to me according to your word." Then the angel departed from her (Luke 1:26–38).

These passages of Scripture record the announcement of the birth of Jesus. It is clearly stated that He would be born of a virgin to fulfill the Old Testament prophecies! We link up the promise in Genesis 3 about the "offspring of the woman" with the prophecy of Isaiah about a child born of a virgin and compare and observe at once that the facts of the birth of Jesus Christ fit in like the pieces of a puzzle. The promised Savior was born of the virgin and He did come to save His people from their sins! Thus the Old Testament begins with a prediction of a Savior who would come to conquer the power of Satan and deal with the problem of sin in human life; the New Testament begins with the record of the actual birth of this Savior. Although there was an element of mystery in the first promise, later predictions and the final fulfillment in the New Testament make the meaning perfectly clear.

THE PROMISE TO ABRAHAM AND HIS DESCENDANTS

The next important promise is found in the story of Abraham. God said to him, *I will bless those who bless you, but the one who treats you lightly I must curse, and all the families of the earth will bless one another by your name* (Genesis 12:3). This promise also seems somewhat vague, for Abraham had a number of sons through Hagar, through Sarah and through Keturah. Later revelations again make it clear that the promised blessing would flow out to the world through

Abraham's son Isaac. Here is the promise as recorded in Genesis: *God said, "No, Sarah your wife is going to bear you a son, and you will name him Isaac. I will confirm my covenant with him as a perpetual covenant for his descendants after him. As for Ishmael, I have heard you. I will indeed bless him, make him fruitful, and give him a multitude of descendants. He will become the father of twelve princes; I will make him into a great nation. But I will establish my covenant with Isaac, whom Sarah will bear to you at this set time next year."* (Genesis 17:19–21). Ishmael was Abraham's firstborn son but He was the son of a secondary wife. Isaac was the son of Sarah, Abraham's principal wife, and God made it very clear that Isaac, not Ishmael would inherit the promises of God.

The same kind of thing was true in the life of Isaac. He also had two sons, Esau and Jacob, but again God revealed that Jacob would be the one to inherit the promises as the channel of Divine blessing. This promise is worded as follows:

and the LORD . . . said, "I am the LORD, the God of your grandfather Abraham and the God of your father Isaac. I will give you and your descendants the ground you are lying on. Your descendants will be like the dust of the earth, and you will spread out to the west, east, north, and south. All the families of the earth will pronounce bless- ings on one another using your name and that of your descendants. (Genesis 28:13–14).

In each case, you will observe, it was God who made the choice of which son should carry forward the Divine purpose and it was God who revealed His will in this matter to the fathers. Once again centuries had to pass before God made clear what He meant by the promise that through those chosen people all nations of the earth would be blessed.

When Jesus Christ was born, the angel announced that this momentous event was *good news that brings great joy to all the people: Today your Savior is born in the city of David. He is Christ the Lord.* (Luke 2:10–11). Thus the promise of worldwide blessing through Abraham was fulfilled in the Messiah (*Christ* is a Greek word meaning the *Messiah*.)

Here then is a common feature of the Old Testament prophecies. First, the prediction is given but what is meant by it was not always very plain to those who first heard it. The prediction is then expanded and explained by other prophecies given hundreds of years later as time moved on toward the day of fulfillment, chosen by God in His almighty wisdom and power.

From the first promise of a Savior, *the offspring of the woman,* the focus narrows to Abraham and his family. It is then narrowed further to the descendants of Jacob. Jacob had twelve sons who founded the twelve tribes of Israel; from these God chose the tribe of Judah to be the Royal tribe. That prediction reads *The scepter will not depart from Judah, nor the ruler's staff from between his feet, until he comes to whom it belongs; the nations will obey him* (Genesis 49:10). Centuries later, God chose David from the tribe of Judah to be the king and then promised him that one of his descendants would reign on an everlasting throne. This important promise reads as follows: *When the time comes for you to die, I will raise up your descendant, one of your own sons, to succeed you, and I will establish his kingdom. He will build a house for my name, and I will make his dynasty permanent. I will become his father and he will become my son. When he sins, I will correct him with the rod of men and with wounds inflicted by human beings. But my loyal love will not be removed from him as I removed it from Saul, whom I removed from before you. Your house and your kingdom will stand before me permanently; your dynasty will be permanent.* " (2 Samuel 7:12–16). Finally, from the family of David it was foretold that the Savior would be born of a virgin!

A SUMMARY

Now let us sum up this list of important predictions. They give the specific details by which this promised Savior was to be recognized when finally He came to earth. We have listed them in order giving first the Old Testament prophecy and then the New Testament fulfillment in the life of Jesus Christ.

Old Testament prediction.	New Testament fulfillment.
Christ would be born in Bethlehem (Micah 5:2).	Jesus was born in Bethlehem (Matthew 2:1–10).
Christ would be preceded by a messenger chosen by God (Malachi 3:1; Isaiah 40:3–5).	Jesus was introduced to Israel by John the Baptist (Matthew 3:3; Mark 1:2; John 1:29).
Christ would be the Foundation on which the New Covenant would be based (Isaiah 28:16).	Jesus is called the Foundation (1 Corinthians 3:11; 1 Peter 2:4–8).
Christ would preach Good News to the world—to all nations (Isaiah 61:1–2; 52:7; 42:6–7; 49:6).	Jesus is the Savior of men (Luke 4:16–21; 24:47; Matthew 28:19–20).

Because of lack of space, we cannot quote all these Scripture passages in full but you can verify them for yourself by looking them up in a Bible.

In summing up this very brief list of some notable predictions, we must refer back to the prophecy of the "New Covenant" which we studied in chapter four. The greatest fact in their national history for the people of Israel was the Covenant made with them by God at the time of Moses. As we have seen Jeremiah 31:31 contains what is perhaps the most astonishing prediction ever to be written by a Hebrew prophet. God said that although the Old Covenant was so inviolably sacred to the Jews, it was to be replaced by a New Covenant. The New Covenant would replace the Old Covenant, not by canceling it, but by fulfilling its purpose. This purpose, as we have seen, was to perfect the plan of salvation for the forgiveness of sin. Who was to be responsible for this truly astonishing departure from the Old Covenant? It was Jesus Christ. He it was who, while instituting a new ceremony, told His followers to take bread and wine as the sign that He had come to bring in the New Covenant! Read His very own words *While they were eating, Jesus took bread, and after giving thanks he broke it, gave it to his disciples, and said, "Take, eat, this is my body." And after taking the cup and giving thanks, he gave it to them, saying, "Drink from it, all of you, for this is my blood, the blood of the covenant, that is poured out for many for the forgiveness of sins. I tell you, from now on I will not drink of this fruit of the vine until that day when I drink it new with you in my Father's kingdom."* (Matthew 26:26–29). Note particularly the words: *"this is my blood, the blood of the covenant, that is poured out for many for the forgiveness of sins."* This is truly a dramatic fulfillment of the prediction made about 600 years earlier. **Jeremiah** foretold the New Covenant; **Jesus** introduced it! **Jeremiah** said its purpose would be to deal with sin; **Jesus** said it was for the remission of sins! The Old Covenant was introduced by **Moses,** the greatest figure in Jewish history. The New Covenant was introduced by **Jesus,** the promised Messiah.

AN IMPORTANT CONCLUSION

Moses was unquestionably great but Jesus is vastly superior and greater than Moses. Examine the following passages of Scripture:

Therefore, holy brothers and sisters, partners in a heavenly calling, take note of Jesus, the apostle and high priest whom we confess, who is faithful to the one who appointed him, as Moses was also in God's house. For he has come to deserve greater glory than Moses, just as the builder of a house deserves greater honor than the house itself! For every house is built by someone, but the builder of all things is God. Now Moses was faithful in all God's house as a servant, to testify to the things that would be spoken. But Christ is faithful as a son over God's house. We are of his house, if in fact we hold firmly to our confidence and the hope we take pride in (Hebrews 3:1–6)

For when Moses had spoken every command to all the people according to the law, he took the blood of calves and goats with water and scarlet wool and hyssop and sprinkled both the book itself and all the people, and said, "This is the blood of the covenant that God has commanded you to keep." And both the tabernacle and all the utensils of worship he likewise sprinkled with blood. Indeed accord-

ing to the law almost everything was purified with blood, and without the shedding of blood there is no forgiveness. So it was necessary for the sketches of the things in heaven to be purified with these sacrifices, but the heavenly things themselves required better sacrifices than these. For Christ did not enter a sanctuary made with hands—the representation of the true sanctuary—but into heaven itself, and he appears now in God's presence for us. And he did not enter to offer himself again and again, the way the high priest enters the sanctuary year after year with blood that is not his own, for then he would have had to suffer again and again since the foundation of the world. But now he has appeared once for all at the consummation of the ages to put away sin by his sacrifice. And just as people are appointed to die once, and then to face judgment, so also, after Christ was offered once to bear the sins of many, to those who eagerly await him he will appear a second time, not to bear sin but to bring salvation. (Hebrews 9:19–28)

Someone who rejected the law of Moses was put to death without mercy on the testimony of two or three witnesses. How much greater punishment do you think that person deserves who has contempt for the Son of God, and profanes the blood of the covenant that made him holy, and insults the Spirit of grace? For we know the one who said, "Vengeance is mine, I will repay," and again, "The LORD will judge his people." It is a terrifying thing to fall into the hands of the living God. (Hebrews 10:28–31).

Any man who despised the Old Covenant of Moses was punished by death, but an infinitely worse judgment will fall upon any one who rejects the New Covenant of Christ. The Old Covenant was confirmed by the blood of an animal sacrifice but the *blood of the Covenant* of Christ was that of the perfect sacrifice of Jesus Himself. With such a clear fulfillment of the Old Testament predictions concerning Christ, we can see how serious is the condition of all those who reject the New Covenant of Jesus. But millions of people still deny that Jesus died as a sacrifice for sin! We will study that problem in the next chapter!

CHAPTER SIX

WHY THE MESSIAH CAME

In the last chapter we saw that God foretold the coming of the Messiah to be the Deliverer and the Savior from sin. Now we must examine some prophecies which have been misunderstood by millions of people despite the fact that the prophecies themselves are quite straightforward. Although all these predictions are found in the Hebrew Scriptures, the Jews somehow formed a completely wrong idea of the purpose of the Messiah's coming. They thought that He would come as a military and political leader to destroy their enemies and establish Jewish sovereignty over all the nations. Because of this belief they rejected Jesus Christ and continue to reject to this day the Christian belief that Jesus is the Messiah. Muslims reject the story of the death of Jesus Christ and the Christian doctrines connected with it. To Muslims, it is impossible to believe that a holy prophet (as they believe Jesus to be) could suffer and die such a cruel and shameful death as crucifixion. There is no point in arguing about such things; we must see what the Bible says.

We cannot form valid opinions of our own about the Messiah, what He would be like and what He would do, unless we realize one thing. It is the Old Testament which tells of the coming of the Messiah. Therefore we must look to the Old Testament to find out what it says about the Messiah. This is the supreme authority on the matter. Does it say that Messiah would be a mighty military conqueror? Does it say that He would come with pomp and majesty? Does it say that He would never suffer defeat? In fact, the prophets foretold some very unexpected facts about the coming Savior.

PROPHECIES ABOUT THE MESSIAH

1. THE MESSIAH WOULD COME IN HUMILITY, NOT WITH POMP AND PRIDE.

Read what Zechariah says, *Rejoice greatly, daughter of Zion! Shout, daughter of Jerusalem! Look! Your king is coming to you: he is legitimate and victorious, humble and riding on a donkey—on a young donkey, the foal of a female donkey* (Zechariah 9:9). Now compare this with what actually happened. *Now when they approached Jerusalem and came to Bethphage, at the Mount of Olives, Jesus sent two disciples, telling them, "Go to the village ahead of you. Right away you will find a donkey tied there, and a colt with her. Untie them and bring them to me. If anyone says anything to you, you are to say, 'The Lord needs them,' and he will send them at once." This took place to fulfill what was spoken by the prophet: "Tell the people of Zion, 'Look, your king is coming to you, unassuming and seated on a donkey, and on a colt, the foal of a donkey.'" So the disciples went and did as Jesus had instructed them. They brought the donkey and the colt and placed their cloaks on them, and he sat on them. A very large crowd spread their cloaks on the road. Others cut branches from the trees and spread them on the road. The crowds that went ahead of him and those following kept shouting, "Hosanna to the Son of David! Blessed is the one who comes in the name of the Lord! Hosanna in the highest!"* (Matthew 21:1–9). Jesus came, not as a military or political leader, but with humility and gentleness. Matthew 11:29 says, *Take my yoke on you and learn from me, because I am gentle and humble in heart, and you will find rest for your souls.*

2. *THE MESSIAH WOULD BE DESPISED AND REJECTED BY MEN.*

The prophet Isaiah foretold, *He was despised and rejected by people, one who experienced pain and was acquainted with illness; people hid their faces from him; he was despised, and we considered him insignificant* (Isaiah 53:3). Jesus was despised and rejected by the Jews. Matthew says:

> *But the chief priests and the elders persuaded the crowds to ask for Barabbas and to have Jesus killed. The governor asked them, "Which of the two do you want me to release for you?" And they said, "Barabbas!" Pilate said to them, "Then what should I do with Jesus who is called the Christ?" They all said, "Crucify him!" He asked, "Why? What wrong has he done?" But they shouted more insistently, "Crucify him!"* (Matthew 27:20–23).

He was also rejected by the Gentiles, the non-Jewish people. We read:

> *Then the governor's soldiers took Jesus into the governor's residence and gathered the whole cohort around him. They stripped him and put a scarlet robe around him, and after braiding a crown of thorns, they put it on his head. They put a staff in his right hand, and kneeling down before him, they mocked him: "Hail, king of the Jews!" They spat on him and took the staff and struck him repeatedly on the head. When they had mocked him, they stripped him of the robe and put his own clothes back on him. Then they led him away to crucify him* (Matthew 27:27–31).

In Psalm 2 it was predicted that kings and rulers and common peoples would unite in rejecting Christ. The fulfillment is recorded in Acts 4:27–28 which says, *For indeed both Herod and Pontius Pilate, with the Gentiles and the people of Israel, assembled together in this city against your holy servant Jesus, whom you anointed, to do as much as your power and your plan had decided beforehand would happen.*

3. THE MESSIAH WOULD BE BETRAYED FOR 30 PIECES OF SILVER.

The prophet Zechariah wrote *Then I said to them, "If it seems good to you, pay me my wages, but if not, forget it." So they weighed out my payment—thirty pieces of silver. The LORD then said to me, "Throw to the potter that exorbitant sum at which they valued me!" So I took the thirty pieces of silver and threw them to the potter at the temple of the LORD* (Zechariah 11:12–13). This was the sum of money paid to Judas to betray Jesus. Matthew tells us, *Then one of the twelve, the one named Judas Iscariot, went to the chief priests and said, "What will you give me to betray him into your hands?" So they set out thirty silver coins for him. From that time on, Judas began looking for an opportunity to betray him.* (Matthew 26:14–16). When Judas saw that Jesus was condemned, he threw the money down in the temple, to be used by the priests for buying the potter's field. We read, *Now when Judas, who had betrayed him, saw that Jesus had been condemned, he regretted what he had done and returned the thirty silver coins to the chief priests and the elders, saying, "I have sinned by betraying innocent blood!" But they said, "What is that to us? You take care of it yourself!" So Judas threw the silver coins into the temple and left. Then he went out and hanged himself. The chief priests took the silver and said, "It is not lawful to put this into the temple treasury, since it is blood money." After consulting together they bought the Potter's Field with it, as a burial place for foreigners. For this reason that field has been called the "Field of Blood" to this day. Then what was spoken by Jeremiah the prophet was fulfilled: "They took the thirty silver coins, the price of the one whose price had been set by the people of Israel, and they gave them for the potter's field, as the Lord commanded me."* (Matthew 27:3–10). This explains the reference made prophetically to the potter's field by Zechariah.

4. THE MESSIAH WOULD BE INSULTED, BEATEN AND SPAT ON.

The Old Testament prophet wrote, *I offered my back to those who attacked, my jaws to those who tore out my beard; I did not hide my face from insults and spitting* (Isaiah 50:6). Jesus was scourged (beaten on the back with a steel-tipped whip), struck in the face and spat upon. The record reads:

> *Then he released Barabbas for them. But after he had Jesus flogged, he handed him over to be crucified. Then the governor's soldiers took Jesus into the governor's residence and gathered the whole cohort around him. They stripped him and put a scarlet robe around him, and after braiding a crown of thorns, they put it on his head. They put a staff in his right hand, and kneeling down before him, they mocked him: "Hail, king of the Jews!" They spat on him and took the staff and struck him repeatedly on the head.* (Matthew 27:26–30).

5. THE MESSIAH WOULD SUFFER AND DIE FOR THE SINS OF OTHERS.

This is clearly stated by the prophet Isaiah, *But he lifted up our illnesses, he carried our pain; even though we thought he was being punished, attacked by God, and afflicted for something he had done. He was wounded because of our rebellious deeds, crushed because of our sins; he endured punishment that made us well; because of his wounds we have been healed. All of us had wandered off like sheep; each of us had strayed off on his own path, but the LORD caused the sin of all of us to attack him. He was treated harshly and afflicted, but he did not even open his mouth. Like a lamb led to the slaughtering block, like a sheep silent before her shearers, he did not even open his mouth* (Isaiah 53:4–7). The whole of the New Testament explains His death was a sacrifice for the sins of mankind. Here are a few examples:

> *Because Christ also suffered once for sins, the just for the unjust, to bring you to God, by being put to death in the flesh but by being made alive in the spirit* (1 Peter 3:18).

> *For I passed on to you as of first importance what I also received—that Christ died for our sins according to the scriptures* (1 Corinthians 15:3).

> *Now he did not say this on his own, but because he was high priest that year, he prophesied that Jesus was going to die for the Jewish nation, and not for the Jewish nation only, but to gather together into one the children of God who are scattered* (John 11:51–52).

6. *THE MESSIAH COULD DIE FOR THE SINS OF OTHERS*
   BECAUSE HE HAD NO SIN OF HIS OWN.

He was sinless. The prophet Isaiah foretold of Him, *They intended to bury him with criminals, but he ended up in a rich man's tomb, because he had committed no violent deeds, nor had he spoken deceitfully* (Isaiah 53:9). The apostle Peter, who had lived with Jesus, wrote, *He committed no sin nor was deceit found in his mouth* (1 Peter 2:22). Thus Christ's death was to be an offering for sin. Isaiah 53:10 says, *Though the LORD desired to crush him and make him ill, once restitution is made, he will see descendants and enjoy long life, and the LORD's purpose will be accomplished through him.* Hebrews 10:12–14 says, *But when this priest had offered one sacrifice for sins for all time, he sat down at the right hand of God where he is now waiting until his enemies are made a footstool for his feet. For by one offering he has perfected for all time those who are made holy.*

7. *THE MESSIAH WOULD DIE BY CRUCIFIXION.*

Crucifixion was not a Jewish form of execution and therefore it is most remarkable that such a form of death would be predicted a thousand years before it took place under the Romans. Yet read this statement from Psalm 22:16, *Yes, wild dogs surround me—a gang of evil men crowd around me; like a lion they pin my hands and feet.* The Messiah would have His hands and feet pierced! In Psalm 34:20 we read, *He protects all his bones; not one of them is broken* When Jesus was crucified all this came true. His hands and feet were nailed to the cross, His side was pierced by a Roman spear, but no bone was broken even though the Roman governor had given orders to break His legs to hasten death. This historical fact is recorded as follows:

> *There they crucified him along with two others, one on each side, with Jesus in the middle* (John 19:18).

> *Then, because it was the day of preparation, so that the bodies should not stay on the crosses on the Sabbath (for that Sabbath was an especially important one), the Jewish leaders asked Pilate to have the victims' legs broken and the bodies taken down. So the soldiers came and broke the legs of the two men who had been crucified with Jesus, first the one and then the other. But when they came to Jesus and saw that he was already dead, they did not break his legs. But one of the soldiers pierced his side with a spear, and blood and water flowed out immediately* (John 19:31–34).

8. THE MESSIAH'S CLOTHING WOULD BE DIVIDED BY GAMBLERS AT HIS DEATH.

Here is what the Old Testament prophet said, *They are dividing up my clothes among themselves; they are rolling dice for my garments* (Psalm 22:18). The fulfillment of this is recorded in Matthew 27:35 which says, *When they had crucified him, they divided his clothes by throwing dice.*

9. THE MESSIAH WOULD DIE IN THE COMPANY OF CRIMINALS.

Isaiah foretold, *So I will assign him a portion with the multitudes, he will divide the spoils of victory with the powerful, because he willingly submitted to death and was numbered with the rebels, when he lifted up the sin of many and intervened on behalf of the rebels* (Isaiah 53:12). Jesus was crucified between two thieves as Mark tells us, *And they crucified two outlaws with him, one on his right and one on his left* (Mark 15:27–28).

10. THE MESSIAH WOULD BE BURIED IN A RICH MAN'S TOMB.

The prophet said, *They intended to bury him with criminals, but he ended up in a rich man's tomb, because he had committed no violent deeds, nor had he spoken deceitfully* (Isaiah 53:9). Normally a crucified person was buried by the Romans in a criminal's grave. But Jesus was placed in a new tomb by Joseph. Matthew tells us what happened:

> *Now when it was evening, there came a rich man from Arimathea, named Joseph, who was also a disciple of Jesus. He went to Pilate and asked for the body of Jesus. Then Pilate ordered that it be given to him. Joseph took the body, wrapped it in a clean linen cloth, and placed it in his own new tomb that he had cut in the rock. Then he rolled a great stone across the entrance of the tomb and went away* (Matthew 27:57–60).

11. THE MESSIAH WOULD RISE FROM THE DEAD.

Psalm 16:10 foretold this in the words: *You will not abandon me to Sheol; you will not allow your faithful follower to see the Pit.* Isaiah also said, *he will swallow up death permanently. The sovereign LORD will wipe away the tears from every face, and remove his people's disgrace from all the earth. Indeed, the LORD has announced it* (Isaiah 25:8). Read the story of what happened in Matthew chapter 28, Mark chapter 16, Luke chapter 24, John chapter 20. Here again the written records are too long to reproduce in their entirety but read them for yourself in your Bible. Peter who knew all these matters first hand says, *For David says about him, 'I saw the Lord always in front of me, for he is at my right hand so that I will not be shaken. Therefore my heart was glad and my tongue rejoiced; my body also will live in hope, because you will not leave my soul in Hades, nor permit your Holy One to experience decay. You have made known to me the paths of life; you will make me full of joy with your presence.' Brothers, I can speak confidently to you about our forefather David, that he both died and was buried, and his tomb is with us to this day. So then, because he was a prophet and knew that God had sworn to him with an oath to seat one of his descendants on his throne, David by foreseeing this spoke about the resurrection of the Christ, that he was neither abandoned to Hades, nor did his body experience decay* (Acts 2:25–31). And Paul, who became convinced of the truth of Christ's resurrection only after he had actually seen the risen Christ himself, says:

> *For I passed on to you as of first importance what I also received— that Christ died for our sins according to the scriptures, and that he was buried, and that he was raised on the third day according to the scriptures, and that he appeared to Cephas, then to the twelve. Then he appeared to more than five hundred of the brothers and sisters at one time, most of whom are still alive, though some have fallen asleep. Then he appeared to James, then to all the apostles* (1 Corinthians 15:3–7).

12. THE MESSIAH WOULD GIVE THE HOLY SPIRIT TO THOSE WHO BELIEVE IN HIM.

The prophet Isaiah foretold this as he did so many other details concerning the Messiah. He said, *The LORD's spirit will rest on him—a spirit that gives extraordinary wisdom, a spirit that provides the ability to execute plans, a spirit that produces absolute loyalty to the LORD. . . . For I will pour water on the parched ground and cause streams to flow on the dry land. I will pour my spirit on your offspring and my blessing on your children* (Isaiah 11:2; 44:3). Jesus, too, promised that He would give the Holy Spirit and did so. John one of His immediate followers says *And after he said this, he breathed on them and said, "Receive the Holy Spirit.* (John 20:22). A short while later, on the day of Pentecost (an annual ancient Jewish religious festival day) the Holy Spirit came as promised. The full story is recorded in Acts 2:1–18 together with a description of what effect this event had on the followers of Jesus and on the people of Jerusalem.

13. THE MESSIAH WOULD SEND HIS MESSAGE OF SALVATION TO ALL NATIONS.

This refers back to the promise in Genesis 22:18, *All the nations of the earth will pronounce blessings on one another using the name of your descendants.* Several Old Testament prophets amplified this theme, Isaiah in particular. He said, *"I, the LORD, officially commission you; I take hold of your hand. I protect you and make you a covenant mediator for people, and a light to the nations, to open blind eyes, to release prisoners from dungeons, those who live in darkness from prisons. . . . he says, 'Is it too insignificant a task for you to be my servant, to reestablish the tribes of Jacob, and restore the remnant of Israel? I will make you a light to the nations, so you can bring my deliverance to the remote regions of the earth.' . . . . 'Arise! Shine! For your light arrives! The splendor of the* LORD *shines on you! For, look, darkness covers the earth and deep darkness covers the nations, but the* LORD *shines on you; his splendor appears over you. . . . For the sake of Zion I will not be silent; for the sake of Jerusalem I will not be quiet, until her vindication shines brightly and her deliverance burns like a torch.'" Nations will see your vindication, and all kings your splendor. You will be called by a new name that the* LORD *himself will give you (Isaiah 42:6–7; 49:6; 60:1–2; 62:1–2).* Now note the words of the Lord Jesus after His resurrection. He said, *Then Jesus came up and said to them, "All authority in heaven and on earth has been given to me. Therefore go and make disciples of all nations, baptizing them in the name of the Father and the Son and the Holy Spirit, teaching them to obey everything I have commanded you. And remember, I am with you always, to the end of the age."* (Matthew 28:18–20). Read also the following Scriptures:

He said to them, "Go into all the world and preach the gospel to every creature" (Mark 16:15).

And repentance for the forgiveness of sins would be proclaimed in his name to all nations, beginning from Jerusalem (Luke 24:47).

But you will receive power when the Holy Spirit has come upon you, and you will be my witnesses in Jerusalem, and in all Judea and Samaria, and to the farthest parts of the earth" (Acts 1:8).

SOME PRACTICAL OBSERVATIONS

These are by no means all the prophecies which could be given for there are many more. These, however, are sufficient to show that predictions made by the prophets centuries before the time of Christ were fulfilled in the death and resurrection of Christ. And, as we have noticed with all the predictions we have studied, when the prophets wrote their predictions, no one could possibly have understood what they really meant; the meaning of the prophecies was made perfectly plain by their obvious fulfillment in the life and death and resurrection of Jesus Christ. The absurd suggestion, made by some, that these prophecies were fabrications intended to deceive people scarcely merits a reply. The Jews themselves, to whom they were given, did not understand their meaning as referring to the coming Messiah so how could they have written them to deceive people?

Let us now summarize the facts briefly. The Old Testament prophets foretold the astonishing fact that the Messiah, when He would finally come to the people of Israel who had expected Him for centuries, would not be recognized by them. He would not fit in with their political aspirations and religious ideas, and so they would reject Him. The fulfillment of this is plainly stated in Acts 13:26–30 where we read:

> *Brothers, descendants of Abraham's family, and those Gentiles among you who fear God, the message of this salvation has been sent to us. For the people who live in Jerusalem and their rulers did not recognize him, and they fulfilled the sayings of the prophets that are read every Sabbath by condemning him. Though they found no basis for a death sentence, they asked Pilate to have him executed. When they had accomplished everything that was written about him, they took him down from the cross and placed him in a tomb. But God raised him from the dead.*

How strange it is that people who profess to believe in the teachings of the holy prophets have failed to understand these amazing predictions which show that the death of Jesus was not a tragic disaster, but was a definite plan which God had foretold in the Scriptures.

The death of Jesus Christ is a fact of history. It was foretold in the writings of the prophets with scores of precise details to make the fulfillment easy to recognize. The fulfillment is recorded in the New Testament by Matthew, Mark, Luke and John who recount the details of the rejection, trial, crucifixion, death, burial and resurrection of Jesus as facts which were witnessed by hundreds of people. The rest of the New Testament, beginning from Acts chapter 2, makes frequent reference to these facts, and explains them as being planned by God in order that men might be saved from sin and set free from the power of Satan.

In spite of this, millions of people still refuse to believe that Jesus died on the cross as a sacrifice for sin. They are thus rejecting the Savior whose coming was promised for thousands of years, with many convincing prophecies all of which were dramatically fulfilled in the few short years that Jesus lived on earth. By refusing to believe the evidence of holy prophets and apostles, men are refusing to believe the word of God, and thus are guilty of the serious sin of rebellion against their Creator. You must either believe or reject God's Word about the Savior. No one can remain neutral in this.

CHAPTER SEVEN

THE MOST IMPORTANT QUESTION OF ALL

As we have examined some of the predictions of the Old Testament and their dramatic fulfillment in the New Testament we have been drawing closer to the most important question of all. What is the truth about Jesus Christ? Why should Jesus become a sacrifice for the sins of other men? The Bible says that He was sinless, while all other men are sinners. But what does this mean? In what way was He different from other men? Muslims believe that all the great prophets were protected from sin, and so they do not accept the claim for the **unique** sinlessness of Jesus.

These are serious matters and we must look to the Bible to discover the truth about them. The subject is really far too extensive to be handled in just a short study. To be fair, when seeking an answer to the mystery of the life of Jesus, we should take time and read the four Gospels—Matthew, Mark, Luke and John—in order to become familiar with the facts. However, even a complete knowledge of the facts will not remove the elements of mystery from our minds. Even the disciples of Jesus, who lived with Him and heard His teaching daily, and watched His miracles, and learned to love Him, were often puzzled by what they saw and heard. Jesus was a man, but He was not like other men! No one, not even His most bitter enemies, ever accused Him of sin. *Who among you can prove me guilty of any sin? If I am telling you the truth, why don't you believe me?* (John 8:46). *Again Pilate went out and said to the Jewish leaders, "Look, I am bringing him out to you, so that you may know that I find no reason for an accusation against him."* (John 19:4). He taught all His followers to confess their sins, but He never confessed sin Himself. But this did not make Him the kind of smug, self-righteous person who is so obnoxious to others. On the contrary, He was called the *"Friend of sinners."* They loved Him. People of all classes were attracted to Him, rich and poor, wise and simple, men, women and children. As we read the narrative, we notice that often even the worst of sinners were transformed into good and godly people as they came to know Him.

Then there was the problem of His astonishing authority. He taught with authority. *They were amazed at his teaching, because he spoke with authority. . . . They were all amazed and began to say to one another, "What's happening here? For with authority and power he commands the unclean spirits, and they come out!"* (Luke 4:32 and 36). He performed miracles with power. He healed blindness, deafness, dumbness and all kinds of sicknesses. He even raised the dead to life. He had power to cast out evil spirits with a word, without incantations. *So a report about him spread throughout Syria. People brought to him all who suffered with various illnesses and afflictions, those who had seizures, paralytics, and those possessed by demons, and he healed them.* (Matthew 4:24). He claimed to have the power to forgive sins, and He proved it.

What kind of a person is this? Guessing or debating will not help. Millions of people have done this for centuries and gained nothing by it. We must examine the facts as the Bible reveals them to us. Christians are not philosophers who invent theories about God and about religious problems. Christians accept what God has revealed in the Bible even though they cannot understand everything.

The mystery surrounding the character and the work of Jesus Christ is explained in the Bible by the fact that Jesus Christ was God revealed in human form. Jews, Muslims and many others deny this emphatically. To do so, they have to deny historically established facts. The Jewish leaders could not deny the claims or the power of Jesus but they rejected Him and had Him crucified to get rid of Him. *So the chief priests and the Pharisees called the council together and said, "What are we doing? For this man is performing many miraculous signs. If we allow him to go on in this way, everyone will believe in him, and the Romans will come and take away our sanctuary and our nation." Then one of them, Caiaphas, who was high priest that year, said, "You know nothing at all! You do not realize that it is more to your advantage to have one man die for the people than for the whole nation to perish." (Now he did not say this on his own, but because he was high priest that year, he prophesied that Jesus was going to die for the Jewish nation, and not for the Jewish nation only, but to gather together into one the children of God who are scattered.) So from that day they planned together to kill him.* (John 11:47–53). *Now a large crowd of Judeans learned that Jesus was there, and so they came not only because of him but also to see Lazarus whom he had raised from the dead. So the chief priests planned to kill Lazarus too, for on account of him many of the Jewish people from Jerusalem were going away and believing in Jesus.* (John 12:9–11). Muslims take the view that the New Testament narratives and the Old Testament prophecies concerning Jesus have been deliberately distorted or invented by evil men. Christians do not deny nor do they reject the truth of the claims of Jesus; they accept them. They cannot explain them, nor can they explain them away, but they accept them as part of the mystery surrounding the Person and work of Christ. Let us face up to these strange claims concerning Jesus Christ. What did He claim about Himself?

1. Jesus claimed that He existed eternally.

> *Jesus said to them, "I tell you the solemn truth, before Abraham came into existence, I am!" (John 8:58). And now, Father, glorify me at your side with the glory I had with you before the world was created* (John 17:5).

2. Jesus claimed to be One with God.

> *"The Father and I are one"* (John 10:30).

> *For this reason the Jewish leaders were trying even harder to kill him, because not only was he breaking the Sabbath, but he was also calling God his own Father, thus making himself equal with God* (John 5:18).

3. Jesus called Himself the "Son of God."

This was supported by the angel Gabriel. *The angel replied, "The Holy Spirit will come upon you, and the power of the Most High will overshadow you. Therefore the child to be born will be holy; he will be called the Son of God"* (Luke 1:35). This was admitted even by evil spirits who cried out in fear in His presence. *Demons also came out of many, crying out, "You are the Son of God!" But he rebuked them, and would not allow them to speak, because they knew that he was the Christ.* (Luke 4:41).

4. JESUS CLAIMED THAT HE CAME TO REVEAL GOD.

Jesus replied, "Have I been with you for so long, and you have not known me, Philip? The person who has seen me has seen the Father! How can you say, 'Show us the Father'?" (John 14:9).

5. JESUS CLAIMED TO HAVE DIVINE POWER.

Then Jesus came up and said to them, "All authority in heaven and on earth has been given to me. Therefore go and make disciples of all nations, baptizing them in the name of the Father and the Son and the Holy Spirit, teaching them to obey everything I have commanded you. And remember, I am with you always, to the end of the age." (Matthew 28:18–20).

6. JESUS CLAIMED TO HAVE POWER TO FORGIVE SINS.

When Jesus saw their faith, he said to the paralytic, "Son, your sins are forgiven. . . . But so that you may know that the Son of Man has authority on earth to forgive sins,"—he said to the paralytic—"I tell you, stand up, take your stretcher, and go home." (Mark 2:5, 10–11).

7. JESUS CLAIMED TO BE THE FINAL JUDGE OF ALL MEN.

Furthermore, the Father does not judge anyone, but has assigned all judgment to the Son (John 5:22). and he has granted the Son authority to execute judgment, because he is the Son of Man (John 5:27).

8. JESUS CLAIMED TO HAVE POWER OVER LIFE AND DEATH.

"I tell you the solemn truth, the one who hears my message and believes the one who sent me has eternal life and will not be condemned, but has crossed over from death to life" (John 5:24).

"For this is the will of my Father—for everyone who looks on the Son and believes in him to have eternal life, and I will raise him up at the last day." (John 6:40).

9. JESUS CLAIMED THE RIGHT TO ACCEPT WORSHIP FROM MEN.

But she came and bowed down before him and said, "Lord, help me!" "It is not right to take the children's bread and throw it to the dogs," he said. "Yes, Lord," she replied, "but even the dogs eat the crumbs that fall from their masters' table." Then Jesus answered her, "Woman, your faith is great! Let what you want be done for you." And her daughter was healed from that hour. (Matthew 15:25–28).

Thomas replied to him, "My Lord and my God!" (John 20:28).

10. *Jesus claimed the right to use names for Himself that were used only for God.*

This is what the LORD, Israel's king, says, their protector, the LORD who leads armies: "I am the first and I am the last, there is no God but me" (Isaiah 44:6).

When I saw him I fell down at his feet as though I were dead, but he placed his right hand on me and said: "Do not be afraid! I am the first and the last" (Revelation 1:17).

We could make this list much longer but ten points are adequate. In fact, had Jesus said only one of these ten things, it would be astonishing. In fact it was these very things that did startle and shock His hearers when He said them. There can be no possible doubt that Jesus made these sweeping claims! For us to deny that He ever said them is simply escapism—a refusal to face facts we consider unpleasant. This was why such a storm of argument, debate, and hatred gathered gradually around Jesus until at last the Jews determined to have Him put to death. Of course, if a man of bad character or a man obviously insane had said such things, the people would have ridiculed him or ignored him. But not even His enemies thought Jesus to be evil or insane. Even atheists will usually admit that the character of Jesus was noble and gracious! He is admired as the finest example of love, kindness, compassion, truth, purity and goodness that the world has ever seen. In fact, it was the unique character and the holy life of Jesus, together with the authority of His teaching and the power of His miracles which compelled His followers to believe His extraordinary claims. His disciples lived with Him, heard His teachings, saw His power, and learned to love and trust Him over a period of more than three years. His disciples were Jews who had memorized, as part of their education, those very qualifications of a True Prophet we examined in a previous chapter.

Jesus passed all the tests and proved His claims to be valid. Yet, so astonishing were the facts, even His most intimate disciples did not fully grasp their implications until Jesus was raised from the dead. The facts connected with His death and resurrection, and the confirmation they found of these in the Old Testament predictions, finally convinced them that Jesus was indeed God manifested in human form. The following verses illustrate how the Lord's apostles expressed their ultimate conviction that His claims to be God in human form were true.

You should have the same attitude toward one another that Christ Jesus had, who though he existed in the form of God did not regard equality with God as something to be grasped, but emptied himself by taking on the form of a slave, by looking like other men, and by sharing in human nature. He humbled himself, by becoming obedient to the point of death —even death on a cross! As a result God exalted him and gave him the name that is above every name, so that at the name of Jesus every knee will bow—in heaven and on earth and under the earth—and every tongue confess that Jesus Christ is Lord to the glory of God the Father. (Philippians 2:5–11). These verses teach that Jesus laid aside the attributes of Deity that He might become Man to save us from sin.

He delivered us from the power of darkness and transferred us to the kingdom of the Son he loves, in whom we have redemption, the forgiveness of sins. He is the image of the invisible God, the firstborn over all creation, for all things in heaven and on earth were created by him—all things, whether visible or invisible, whether thrones or dominions, whether principalities or powers—all things were created through him and for him. He himself is before all things and all things are held together in him. He is the head of the body, the church, as well as the beginning, the firstborn from among the dead, so that he himself may become first in all things. For God was pleased to have all his fullness dwell in the Son and through him to reconcile all things to himself by making peace through the blood of his cross—through him, whether things on earth or things in heaven. (Colossians 1:13–20). These verses show that Jesus, the Son of God, was creator of all, and yet He became the Savior of sinners.

After God spoke long ago in various portions and in various ways to our ancestors through the prophets, in these last days he has spoken to us in a son, whom he appointed heir of all things, and through whom he created the world. The Son is the radiance of his glory and the representation of his essence, and he sustains all things by his powerful word, and so when he had accomplished cleansing for sins, he sat down at the right hand of the Majesty on high. (Hebrews 1:1–3). Jesus is here described as being the *"representation of his essence"* (the original word signifies "character") of God and that He came as the final messenger to save sinners.

In the beginning was the Word, and the Word was with God, and the Word was fully God. The Word was with God in the beginning. All things were created by him, and apart from him not one thing was created that has been created. In him was life, and the life was the light of mankind. And the light shines on in the darkness, but the darkness has not mastered it. A man came, sent from God, whose name was John. He came as a witness to testify about the light, so that everyone might believe through him. He himself was not the light, but he came to testify about the light. The true light, who gives light to everyone, was coming into the world. He was in the world, and the world was created by him, but the world did not recognize him. He came to what was his own, but his own people did not receive him. But to all who have received him—those who believe in his name—he has given the right to become God's children— children not born by human parents or by human desire or a husband's decision, but by God. Now the Word became flesh and took up residence among us. We saw his glory—the glory of the one and only, full of grace and truth, who came from the Father. John testified about him and shouted out, "This one was the one about whom I said, 'He who comes after me is greater than I am, because he existed before me.'" For we have all received from his fullness one gracious gift after another. For the law was given through Moses, but grace and truth came about through Jesus Christ. No one has ever seen God. The only one, himself God, who is in closest fellowship with the Father, has made God known. (John 1:1–18). Jesus was God; He was Creator; He became the Savior.

Many additional verses point to the same essential facts concerning Jesus. Let us summarize these facts. The Old Testament predictions said that the Messiah was God. The New Testament narrative contains His own claims to be God. The apostles believed Jesus to be God. The teachings and the miracles, the life and the character, the death and the resurrection of Jesus all point in the same direction. Jesus Christ was God manifested in human form to save us.

In view of such an array of facts, why do so many people still violently reject this claim? There is a reason for this. If Jesus is "Son of God," then what about the basic doctrine of the Unity of God, held loyally by Jews and Muslims? Remember, Christians are just as staunchly monotheistic as Jews and Muslims; they firmly believe that God is **One.** However, they hold also to the Biblical doctrine of the Trinity for God has revealed Himself as **One Trinity,** Father-Son-Holy Spirit, Three-in-one God. There is a mystery about this concept of God which we shall now try to explain. Christians did not invent this belief nor did they choose it because they thought it was a "better" concept of what God is like! Christians accept the idea of the Trinity because this is the only way to account for the mystery of the Godhead.

The doctrine of the Trinity is not (as some people ignorantly suppose) that God + Jesus + Holy Spirit = three Gods. Such a teaching would indeed be an attack upon the Unity of God. The doctrine of the Trinity is that from all eternity God has existed in a Three-fold Oneness, which owing to the limitations of human thought and language must be described as Father-Son-Spirit = God Almighty. To put it another way, Jews, Muslims and others accept a Unitarian Concept of Absolute Unity, while Christians accept a Trinitarian Concept of Compound Unity. This concept is not as difficult to grasp as it appears. It can be demonstrated by a very simple diagram, as follows:

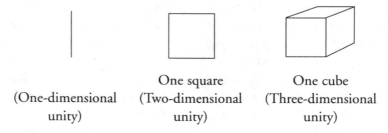

	One square	One cube
(One-dimensional	(Two-dimensional	(Three-dimensional
unity)	unity)	unity)

A cube is obviously three-dimensional, yet it is still one object! This illustration helps us understand the Bible description of an

Almighty God who is immeasurably greater than Man, His creature. It is far more satisfying to our faith and our reason to conceive of Him as a Perfect, Infinite Three-in-one Fullness than to conceive of Him as an Abstract Unity. Thus when this Almighty God willed to reveal Himself to sinful mankind, He chose to do so in human form, Jesus (God the Son) revealing God the Father by the power of God the Holy Spirit. Please note that no Christian, anywhere or at any time, has ever believed that the Trinity consists of God—Virgin Mary—Jesus, as some Muslims think!

The Bible does not teach that a person must understand the mystery of the Trinity before he or she can be saved from sin. Jesus plainly taught that no man can possibly understand the mystery of the "Father" and the "Son," but that when a sinner comes to Jesus Christ in sincere faith, Jesus reveals the truth about the Father to him. *All things have been handed over to me by my Father. No one knows the Son except the Father, and no one knows the Father except the Son and anyone to whom the Son decides to reveal him* (Matthew 11:27).

The apostles also taught in this same practical way. They never attempted to formulate a "doctrine of the Trinity" but they did teach the necessity of knowing God through Jesus Christ. Read the following extracts from their preaching: *Peter said to them, "Repent, and each one of you be baptized in the name of Jesus Christ for the forgiveness of your sins, and you will receive the gift of the Holy Spirit. For the promise is for you and your children, and for all who are far away, as many as the Lord our God will call to himself"* (Acts 2:38–39). *The God of our forefathers raised up Jesus, whom you seized and killed by hanging him on a tree. God exalted him to his right hand as Leader and Savior, to give repentance to Israel and forgiveness of sins. And we are witnesses of these events, and so is the Holy Spirit whom God has given to those who obey him* (Acts 5:30–32). *But Stephen, full of the Holy Spirit, looked intently toward heaven and saw the glory of God, and Jesus standing at the right hand of God. "Look!" he said. "I see the heavens opened, and the Son of Man standing at the right hand of God!"* (Acts 7:55–56). Notice how the apostles explained that through personal faith and trust in Jesus as Savior, the Holy Spirit came into their lives, and this made fellowship with God a reality. Or in other words, salvation from sin is the work of One God, who can only be understood fully through the three-fold revelation of His character as Father-Son-Spirit. This truth is not grasped mentally, but it is made real in an experiential oneness with this Almighty loving God and Savior.

Faith in Christ does not create a conflict of loyalties. A pagan might worship three gods who compete for his worship but the Father the Son and the Spirit are not like that. They are one God. Faith in Christ brings us into an experience of living relationship with a God of love and grace who has taken away the barrier of our sin. Faith in Christ brings us into vital union with God the Father, God the Son and God the Spirit, the one Eternal God of love and truth.

Jesus said, *Now this is eternal life—that they know you, the only true God, and Jesus Christ, whom you sent* (John 17:3).

Do you **know** God, or is He to you the Great Unknowable, Impersonal Creator?

CHAPTER EIGHT

THE FINAL MESSENGER

As we have seen the Bible reveals the unique nature of Jesus. He cannot be explained in terms of normal human life and personality; He is God self-revealed in human form for the purpose of saving His creatures from their sin. Because of this, His authority over men is absolute and final. In unmistakable language, the Bible teaches the complete finality of Christ.

JESUS CHRIST IS THE FINAL MESSENGER TO MANKIND

In Hebrews 1:1–3 we read, *After God spoke long ago in various portions and in various ways to our ancestors through the prophets, in these last days he has spoken to us in a son, whom he appointed heir of all things, and through whom he created the world. The Son is the radiance of his glory and the representation of his essence, and he sustains all things by his powerful word, and so when he had accomplished cleansing for sins, he sat down at the right hand of the Majesty on high.* In the periods prior to the coming of Christ, God spoke to men in many different ways through His messengers. Sometimes His Word was conveyed to the prophets in visions and dreams, sometimes by means of an audible voice, and sometimes through angels. But because, in every case, the prophet was an ordinary human being with limited knowledge and capacity, the fullness of Divine Truth could never be perfectly expressed. The prophets had wonderful glimpses of the power, the wisdom, the holiness and the glory of God, but their knowledge was fragmentary and imperfect. In order to present a perfect revelation of the truth about God, after all the prophets had done their work, God spoke finally through Jesus Christ. God has spoken in these last days through His Son.

Remember, Jesus is never called "Son of God" in a carnal or fleshly sense! He did not become Son of God because He was born of the Virgin Mary. He was the **eternal** Son of God, a member of the Trinity as we saw in the last chapter. The notion that there was anything in the nature of a carnal union between God and the Virgin Mary in order to beget a Son is false and blasphemous. And yet millions of people have been taught that Christians believe such a thing! By a unique miracle, Jesus was born of Mary, in order that He might enter human life as the Savior. He is called "Son of God" and "Son of Man" in the Bible to indicate His unique nature. In some religions, for instance Hinduism, there are stories of the gods taking human form, in a kind of "incarnation" which is vague, shadowy and unreal—in fact more of a "materialization" than an incarnation. But Jesus literally came in human form. Read the following: *So when he came into the world, he said, "Sacrifice and offering you did not desire, but a body you prepared for me. "Whole burnt offerings and sin-offerings you took no delight in." Then I said, "Here I am: I have come—it is written of me in the scroll of the book—to do your will, O God."* (Hebrews 10:5–7). Note especially the words *a body you prepared for me.* Read also Galatians 4:4, *But when the appropriate time had come, God sent out his Son, born of a woman, born under the law.* Never make the mistake of thinking that Jesus was a man who "became God." He was God who "became Man"—a totally different thing!

The Bible speaks of The Eternal Father, The Eternal Son, and The Eternal Spirit, so it is folly to imagine that Jesus "became" the Son of God at birth. Because of the truth of this fact concerning the nature and eternal Deity of Jesus Christ, it is obvious why He has to be the Final Messenger from God to men. He came to bring a perfect revelation of the love and power of God. Human minds cannot really grasp the character of God. But we do know, in some measure, about love, grace, compassion, mercy, power, holiness, immortality and infinitude. The Lord Jesus revealed God's character along all these lines. We can know what God is like by looking at His Son and listening to Him.

Human beings, being limited to the impressions gained by their five senses, find it impossible to understand invisible realities and spiritual truths in an abstract way. For this reason, Jesus constantly taught by means of parables. A parable is a story in terms we **do** understand, which explains truths we **do not** understand. Here is one of the most important parables that Jesus told.

Listen to another parable: There was a landowner who planted a vineyard. He put a fence around it, dug a pit for its winepress, and built a watchtower. Then he leased it to tenant farmers and went on a journey. When the harvest time was near, he sent his slaves to the tenants to collect his portion of the crop. But the tenants seized his slaves, beat one, killed another, and stoned another. Again he sent other slaves, more than the first, and they treated them the same way. Finally he sent his son to them, saying, 'They will respect my son.' But when the tenants saw the son, they said to themselves, 'This is the heir. Come, let's kill him and get his inheritance!' So they seized him, threw him out of the vineyard, and killed him. Now when the owner of the vineyard comes, what will he do to those tenants?" They said to him, "He will utterly destroy those evil men! Then he will lease the vineyard to other tenants who will give him his portion at the harvest." Jesus said to them, "Have you never read in the scriptures: 'The stone the builders rejected has become the cornerstone. This is from the Lord, and it is marvelous in our eyes'? For this reason I tell you that the kingdom of God will be taken from you and given to a people who will produce its fruit. The one who falls on this stone will be broken to pieces, and the one on whom it falls will be crushed." When the chief priests and the Pharisees heard his parables, they realized that he was speaking about them. They wanted to arrest him, but they were afraid of the crowds, because the crowds regarded him as a prophet (Matthew 21:33–46).

The actual story is easy to understand. Here is the meaning behind it. God had sent His servants the holy prophets to teach Israel the truth about the kind of "harvest" God wanted from men-goodness, truth, purity, love, worship and devotion. Instead of obeying the Word of God, Israel despised the prophets and persecuted them and sometimes even killed them. (This is a simple fact of history, examples of which are recorded in the Old Testament.) Now notice the words in the parable, *"Finally he sent his son"*! Jesus, the Son of God is the last of all the messengers to mankind. In the parable, the wicked men killed the son. When Jesus came men crucified Him! The story goes on to show that no other messengers will be sent! Those who rejected and despised Jesus will be punished by God. To reject God's Final Messenger is to reject God Himself.

JESUS CHRIST IS THE FINAL MESSENGER BECAUSE HE IS ALIVE!

He died and rose again and is for evermore a living Savior whose power can never be changed, canceled, abrogated or superseded by any other human being. His power is called *the power of an indestructible life. Who has become a priest not by a legal regulation about physical descent but by the power of an indestructible life* (Hebrews 7:16). *And by being perfected in this way, he became the source of eternal salvation to all who obey him* (Hebrews 5:9). Every other prophet, every other teacher, every other leader lived and died and other men carried on the work they began. But Jesus, alive from the dead, lives forever and is *able to save completely those who come to God through him, because he always lives to intercede for them* (Hebrews 7:25). Jesus claims this Himself. Read His own words: *When I saw him I fell down at his feet as though I were dead, but he placed his right hand on me and said: "Do not be afraid! I am the first and the last, and the one who lives! I was dead, but look, now I am alive—forever and ever—and I hold the keys of death and of Hades!"* (Revelation 1:17–18). Could anything be more final than that? Jesus is the Last one! Who has power to save us from sin—dead prophets, or a Savior who died and rose from among the dead and lives forever? Whom should we love and trust—prophets or the living Savior who holds the keys of hell and of death? The resurrection of Christ is the fact that gives Him the place of absolute finality.

It is important that we read 1 Corinthians 15 at this stage (verse numbers have been included for convenience).

¹ Now I want to make clear for you, brothers and sisters, the gospel that I preached to you, that you received and on which you stand, ² and by which you are being saved, if you hold firmly to the message I preached to you—unless you believed in vain. ³ For I passed on to you as of first importance what I also received—that Christ died for our sins according to the scriptures, ⁴ and that he was buried, and that he was raised on the third day according to the scriptures, ⁵ and that he appeared to Cephas, then to the twelve. ⁶ Then he appeared to more than five hundred of the brothers and sisters at one time, most of whom are still alive, though some have fallen asleep. *7* Then he appeared to James, then to all the apostles. *8* Last of all, as though to one born at the wrong time, he appeared to me also. *9* For I am the least of the apostles, unworthy to be called an apostle, because I persecuted the church of God. *10* But by the grace of God I am what I am, and his grace to me has not been in vain. In fact, I worked harder than all of them—yet not I, but the grace of God with me. *11* Whether then it was I or they, this is the way we preach and this is the way you believed. *12* Now if Christ is being preached as raised from the dead, how can some of you say there is no resurrection of the dead? *13* But if there is no resurrection of the dead, then not even Christ has been raised. *14* And if Christ has not been raised, then our preaching is futile and your faith is empty. *15* Also, we are found to be false witnesses about God, because we have testified against God that he raised Christ from the dead, when in reality he did not raise him, if indeed the dead are not raised. *16* For if the dead are not raised, then not even Christ has been raised. *17* And if Christ has not been raised, your faith is useless; you are still in your sins. *18* Furthermore, those who have fallen asleep in Christ have also perished. *19* For if only in this life we have hope in Christ, we should be pitied more than anyone. *20* But now Christ has been raised from the dead, the firstfruits of those who have fallen asleep. *21* For since death came through a man, the resurrection of the dead also came through a man. *22* For just as in Adam all die, so also in Christ all will be made alive. *23* But each in his own order: Christ, the first-fruits; then when Christ comes, those who belong to him. *24* Then comes the end, when he hands over the kingdom to God the Father, when he has brought to an end all rule and all authority and power. *25* For he must reign until he has put all his enemies under his feet. *26* The last enemy to be eliminated is death. *27* For he has put everything in subjection under his feet. But when it says "everything" has been put in subjection, it is clear that this does not include the one who put everything in subjection to him. *28* And when all things are subjected to him, then the Son himself will be subjected to the one who subjected everything to him, so that God may be all in all. *29*

Otherwise, what will those do who are baptized for the dead? If the dead are not raised at all, then why are they baptized for them? **30** *Why too are we in danger every hour?* **31** *Every day I am in danger of death! This is as sure as my boasting in you, which I have in Christ Jesus our Lord.* **32** *If from a human point of view I fought with wild beasts at Ephesus, what did it benefit me? If the dead are not raised, let us eat and drink, for tomorrow we die.* **33** *Do not be deceived: "Bad company corrupts good morals."* **34** *Sober up as you should, and stop sinning! For some have no knowledge of God—I say this to your shame!* **35** *But someone will say, "How are the dead raised? With what kind of body will they come?"* **36** *Fool! What you sow will not come to life unless it dies.* **37** *And what you sow is not the body that is to be, but a bare seed—perhaps of wheat or something else.* **38** *But God gives it a body just as he planned, and to each of the seeds a body of its own.* **39** *All flesh is not the same: People have one flesh, animals have another, birds and fish another.* **40** *And there are heavenly bodies and earthly bodies. The glory of the heavenly body is one sort and the earthly another.* **41** *There is one glory of the sun, and another glory of the moon and another glory of the stars, for star differs from star in glory.* **42** *It is the same with the resurrection of the dead. What is sown is perishable, what is raised is imperishable.* **43** *It is sown in dishonor, it is raised in glory; it is sown in weakness, it is raised in power;* **44** *it is sown a natural body, it is raised a spiritual body. If there is a natural body, there is also a spiritual body.* **45** *So also it is written, "The first man, Adam, became a living person"; the last Adam became a life-giving spirit.* **46** *However, the spiritual did not come first, but the natural, and then the spiritual.* **47** *The first man is from the earth, made of dust; the second man is from heaven.* **48** *Like the one made of dust, so too are those made of dust, and like the one from heaven, so too those who are heavenly.* **49** *And just as we have borne the image of the man of dust, let us also bear the image of the man of heaven.* **50** *Now this is what I am saying, brothers and sisters: Flesh and blood cannot inherit the kingdom of God, nor does the perishable inherit the imperishable.* **51** *Listen, I will tell you a mystery: We will not all sleep, but we will all be changed—* **52** *in a moment, in the blinking of an eye,* *at the last trumpet. For the trumpet will sound, and the dead will be raised imperishable, and we will be changed. 53 For this perishable body must put on the imperishable, and this mortal body must put on immortality. 54 Now when this perishable puts on the imperishable, and this mortal puts on immortality, then the saying that is written will happen, "Death has been swallowed up in victory." 55 "Where, O death, is your victory? Where, O death, is your sting?" 56 The sting of death is sin, and the power of sin is the law. 57 But thanks be to God, who gives us the victory through our Lord Jesus Christ! 58 So then, dear brothers and sisters, be firm. Do not be moved! Always be outstanding in the work of the Lord, knowing that your labor is not in vain in the Lord.*

The apostle Paul lists some of the striking facts about the resurrection of Christ from the dead. Notice the following points:

a. The resurrection was foretold in the Old Testament (verse 3).
b. It was verified by hundreds of witnesses (verses 5–8).
c. It is the guarantee that true believers in him will rise from the dead (verses 16–22).
d. It explains how the dead will be raised up (verses 35–49).

One striking fact in these verses is the contrast made between Adam and Jesus. What does this mean? Adam was the first man on earth and was therefore the federal head of the human race. He was created by a Divine miracle and appointed to govern the earth for God. But as we have seen in earlier chapters, Adam sinned, and every human being has inherited as a result a sinful human nature which brings death. Paul puts it this way: *So then, just as sin entered the world through one man and death through sin, and so death spread to all people because all sinned* (Romans 5:12). To fulfill God's promise Jesus came into the world to deal with sin and its effects in human life. He was born of the Virgin Mary by a special Divine miracle so that He might become the Head of a new race of spiritual men and women whose sins have been forgiven. From Adam to Jesus, death reigned over all men, but Jesus overcame death and rose from among the dead. The contrast is made very clear. Adam, the first head of the **natural** human race, brought sin and death to man. Jesus, Head of the new **spiritual** "race," composed of those who receive eternal life, has *has broken the power of death and brought life and immortality to light* (2 Timothy 1:10). Adam was tempted by Satan and caused sin to enter human experience (Genesis 3). Jesus was tempted by Satan but did not sin (Matthew 4:1–11) and thus is qualified to be the Savior of sinners.

Adam was created as a living person, but Jesus is a *life-giving Spirit* (Corinthians 15:45), who has the power to give eternal life to all who trust Him as Savior. John says, *I give them eternal life, and they will never perish; no one will snatch them from my hand* (John 10:28). This is why we find the expressions "The first Adam" and "the last Adam" (Jesus). Through the first Adam we all inherit mortal life and a sinful nature. Through the last Adam we all may inherit eternal life. Notice the importance of 1 Corinthians 15:50 which makes it clear that "flesh and blood" (mere human nature) can never inherit the kingdom of God. Then how may we enter that glorious spiritual and everlasting kingdom? The answer is given by Jesus Himself—

> *Jesus replied, "I tell you the solemn truth, unless a person is born from above, he cannot see the kingdom of God" (John 3:3). But to all who have received him—those who believe in his name—he has given the right to become God's children —children not born by human parents or by human desire or a husband's decision, but by God (John 1:12–13).*

JESUS CHRIST IS THE FINAL MESSENGER BECAUSE HE IS COMING AGAIN!

Every other prophet fulfilled his service for God and then died, and new prophets were raised up to speak God's Word. Death brought their work to an end. But Jesus died and rose from among the dead and went into the presence of God where He is today as a living Savior. Other prophets were simply human instruments by which God gave His Word to the world, but Jesus is Himself "The Word of God." As you read the following verses remember that "the Word" is one of the great Names of Jesus. He is not just a "messenger with God's words"; He is "The Word of God"!

In the beginning was the Word, and the Word was with God, and the Word was fully God. The Word was with God in the beginning. All things were created by him, and apart from him not one thing was created that has been created. In him was life, and the life was the light of mankind. And the light shines on in the darkness, but the darkness has not mastered it. A man came, sent from God, whose name was John. He came as a witness to testify about the light, so that everyone might believe through him. He himself was not the light, but he came to testify about the light. The true light, who gives light to everyone, was coming into the world. He was in the world, and the world was created by him, but the world did not recognize him. He came to what was his own, but his own people did not receive him. But to all who have received him—those who believe in his name—he has given the right to become God's children—children not born by human parents or by human desire or a husband's decision, but by God. Now the Word became flesh and took up residence among us. We saw his glory—the glory of the one and only, full of grace and truth, who came from the Father. John testified about him and shouted out, "This one was the one about whom I said, 'He who comes after me is greater than I am, because he existed before me.'" For we have all received from his fullness one gracious gift after another. For the law was given through Moses, but grace and truth came about through Jesus Christ. No one has ever seen God. The only one, himself God, who is in closest fellowship with the Father, has made God known. (John 1:1–18).

Even in the Quran Jesus is called "Kalimat'ullah"—the Word of God! Could "The Word of God" be untrue? Could God's Word be false? Impossible! It is thus of tremendous importance to see that this "Faithful Witness" Himself said that He is coming again to this earth! In John 14:3 He said, *I will come again.* In Acts 1:11 an angel repeated the same message! *Men of Galilee, why do you stand here looking up into the sky? This same Jesus who has been taken up from you into heaven will come back in the same way you saw him go into heaven.* In about 300 places in the New Testament there are references to the fact of the coming of Christ the second time!

Of course there are many predictions about this fact in the Old Testament also. It was this aspect of prophecy which confused the Jews. They were enthusiastic about the prophecies which foretold the coming of Christ in power and glory, but they had overlooked the clear predictions which foretold that at His first coming to earth He would suffer, die and live again. At the end of this age, He is coming back. Luke says, *So he said to them, "You foolish people—how slow of heart to believe all that the prophets have spoken! Wasn't it necessary for the Christ to suffer these things and enter into his glory?" Then beginning with Moses and all the prophets, he interpreted to them the things written about himself in all the scriptures* (Luke 24:25–27). He came once to die for our sins; He will come again to reward all those who love and obey Him and to punish those who reject Him. Here is an important statement about that: *And to you who are being afflicted to give rest together with us when the Lord Jesus is revealed from heaven with his mighty angels. With flaming fire he will mete out punishment on those who do not know God and do not obey the gospel of our Lord Jesus. They will undergo the penalty of eternal destruction, away from the presence of the Lord and from the glory of his strength, when he comes to be glorified among his saints and admired on that day among all who have believed —and you did in fact believe our testimony* (2 Thessalonians 1:7–10). This great Savior is coming again that is certain. Peter says, *Dear friends, this is already the second letter I have written you, in which I am trying to stir up your pure mind by way of reminder: I want you to recall both the predictions foretold by the holy prophets and the commandment of the Lord and Savior through your apostles. Above all, understand this: In the last days blatant scoffers will come, being propelled by their own evil urges and saying, "Where is his promised return? For ever since our ancestors died, all things have continued as they were from the beginning of creation." For they deliberately suppress this fact, that by the word of God heavens existed long ago and an earth was formed out of water and by means of water. Through these things the world existing at that time was destroyed when it was deluged with water. But by the same word the present heavens and earth have been reserved for fire, by being kept for the day of judgment and destruction of the ungodly. Now, dear friends, do not let this one thing escape your notice, that a single day is like a thousand years with the Lord and a thousand years are like a single day. The Lord is not slow concerning his promise, as some regard slowness, but is being patient toward you, because he does not wish for any to perish but for all to come to repentance. But the day of the Lord will come like a thief; when it comes, the heavens will disappear with a horrific noise, and the celestial bodies will melt away in a blaze, and the earth and every deed done on it will be laid bare. Since all these things are to melt away in this manner, what sort of people must we be, conducting our lives in holiness and godliness, while waiting for and hastening the coming of the day of God? Because of this day, the heavens will be burned up and dissolve, and the celestial bodies will melt away in a blaze! But, according to his promise, we are waiting for new heavens and a new earth, in which righteousness truly resides. Therefore, dear friends, since you are waiting for these things, strive to be found at peace, without spot or blemish, when you come into his presence. And regard the patience of our Lord as salvation, just as also our dear brother Paul wrote to you, according to the wisdom given to him, speaking of these things in all his letters. Some things in these letters are hard to understand, things the ignorant and unstable twist to their own destruction, as they also do to the rest of the scriptures. Therefore, dear friends, since you have been forewarned, be on your guard that you do not get led astray by the error of these unprincipled men and fall from your firm grasp on the truth. But grow in the grace and knowledge of our Lord and Savior Jesus Christ. To him be the honor both now and on that eternal day.* (2 Peter 3). What will the return of Jesus mean to you? Will you rejoice to see Him and welcome Him as a Savior you have loved and obeyed, or will you tremble as an unbeliever because you rejected Him and mocked at His claims to be the Final Messenger to mankind?

Toward the end of the Bible we read of a vision God gave to the apostle John concerning the final judgment. It says, *Then I saw heaven opened and here came a white horse! The one riding it was called "Faithful" and "True," and with justice he judges and goes to war. His eyes are like a fiery flame and there are many diadem crowns on his head. He has a name written that no one knows except himself. He is dressed in clothing dipped in blood, and he is called the Word of God. The armies that are in heaven, dressed in white, clean, fine linen, were following him on white horses. From his mouth extends a sharp sword, so that with it he can strike the nations. He will rule them with an iron rod, and he stomps the winepress of the furious wrath of God, the All-Powerful. He has a name written on his clothing and on his thigh: "King of kings and Lord of lords.* (Revelation 19:11–16). Who is the One coming to judge mankind? His Name is called "The Word of God" and He is seen as KING OF KINGS AND LORD OF LORDS.

What tremendous issues depend upon your attitude to Jesus Christ now! You are determining your eternal relationship to God's Son.

CHAPTER NINE

THE SIN QUESTION

In every land, in every culture and every religion we find that men have certain ideas of what is right and what is wrong. These ideas vary considerably, so that something which one man calls "virtue" is called "vice" by others. A pagan savage may throw his baby to the crocodiles as a sacrifice, thinking this is a virtuous act which pleases his gods, but to us, the same act is classed as murder. For this reason, the question, "What is sin?" is very important. How can we know right from wrong?

The Bible is our source of true knowledge about sin; it is indeed a textbook on the subject. No one can read the Bible without realizing that the subject of sin is raised on almost every page. Other books deal with sin and how it can be forgiven, but the Bible is unique. For one thing, it does not minimize the seriousness of sin, but describes its results in plain language. Some people think the Bible has too much to say about sin—they say that it is not suitable for reading in public! Such people often overlook the fact that the Bible never talks about sin merely to entertain evil-minded sensation-hunters, but always to show the awful effects of sin in human life. Sin is shown to be harmful to man and hateful to God.

THE ORIGIN OF SIN

God created man without sin. In the account of the creation of man we read that God saw that all He had made was very good. Adam and Eve lived in a state of happiness and purity and in perfect fellowship with God. We do not know how long this state of innocence lasted but we do know how it was lost, for the story is found in Genesis 3. It was disobedience to God's will which brought sin into human experience. This brings us to the first important fact. God is not responsible for human sin, man is!

The story of the creation of man shows that God gave man the right to choose. Free-will is an essential part of human nature and it was God the Creator who gave the power of choice to man and so long as man chose to obey God, he enjoyed peace and purity. Sin came into human life as a result of self-will and disobedience. The circumstances of the first act of sin are these. Satan came to Adam and Eve and tempted them to distrust God. He suggested that God was preventing them from enjoying the full benefits of life, and that if they disobeyed God's law they would be much happier. He promised that they would become like gods, knowing the difference between good and evil. They would have a new experience; they would increase their knowledge. There was an element of truth in what Satan said. In the very act of disobedience they did enter into a new experience—they learned to know what evil was! Until that time they had known only goodness and happiness, but now they had the knowledge of evil which always brings sorrow in its train. Thus sin became a reality in human life. *So then, just as sin entered the world through one man and death through sin, and so death spread to all people because all sinned* (Romans 5:12). The human race was corrupted at its source. If a spring is corrupt, then all the water from it is bound to be impure. Sin is part of our natural inheritance. Men hate this teaching of the Bible about sin; they hate to be told that they have a sinful nature, Let us see if this is really true.

A DEFINITION OF SIN

Before going any further, we must read several passages of Scripture:

And the LORD passed by before him and proclaimed: "The LORD, the LORD, the compassionate and gracious God, slow to anger, and abounding in loyal love and faithfulness, keeping loyal love for thousands, forgiving iniquity, and transgression and sin. But he by no means leaves the guilty unpunished, visiting the iniquity of the fathers on the children and on the children's children, to the third and fourth generation." (Exodus 34:6–7).

How happy is the one whose rebellious acts are forgiven, whose sin is pardoned! How happy is the one whose wrongdoing the Lord does not punish, in whose spirit there is no deceit. When I refused to confess my sin, my whole body wasted away, while I groaned in pain all day long. For day and night you tormented me; you tried to destroy me in the intense heat of summer. Then I confessed my sin; I no longer covered up my wrongdoing. I said, "I will confess my rebellious acts to the LORD." And then you forgave my sins (Psalm 32:1–5).

Have mercy on me, O God, because of your loyal love! Because of your great compassion, wipe away my rebellious acts! Scrub away my wrongdoing! Cleanse me of my sin! For I am aware of my rebellious acts; I am forever conscious of my sin. Against you, especially you, I have sinned; I have done what is sinful in your sight. So you are just when you confront me; you are right when you condemn me (Psalm 51:1–4).

In these quotations we find three words used to describe the condition of our hearts and our daily behavior as seen by God.

1. *INIQUITY*

This word comes from a root meaning "to bend or twist." The modern word which conveys the same meaning is our word "perversion." The Bible states that in the sight of a holy God, human nature is crooked, twisted, perverted. We know what is the right thing to do, but because of a "twist" in our nature, we constantly do the wrong things. This shows us that sin is more than a wrong act—it comes from a distorted, unbalanced attitude in human nature.

2. *REBELLION (TRANSGRESSION)*

This word means to cross over a line, to deliberately disobey a law. From the very beginning, human sin was rebellion against God's laws. Whenever we sin, we do so with the knowledge that it is wrong and therefore we must accept personal responsibility for our actions.

3. *SIN*

This little word means "to come short," to fail to reach a standard. We know that God is holy and that His laws are good and that He desires us to obey Him, but we never reach His standard of constant obedience. No man is ever as good as he knows he ought to be, *For all have sinned and fall short of the glory of God* (Romans 3:23).

These words teach us that man is perverted in his thoughts, motives and actions, that he deliberately transgresses God's laws, and is incapable of reaching the standard of perfect holiness which God requires.

This Biblical teaching aims a devastating blow to man's pride and because of this many people refuse to believe what the Bible says about sin. Modern man is proud of his intellectual and technical prowess and hates to be told that God sees him as a sinner. But this only proves the Bible to be true. Human nature is so twisted by sin that we pretend that we are good enough to please God and win His favor by our own merit. It was for this very reason that God gave His laws to mankind. Any honest person can test himself in five minutes on this. Read the Ten Commandments carefully:

And God spoke all these words: I, the LORD, am your God, who brought you from the land of Egypt, from the house of bondage. You shall have no other gods before me. You shall not make for yourself a carved image or any likeness of anything that is in heaven above, or that is on earth under it, or that is in the water below. You shall not bow down to them or serve them, for I, the LORD, your God, am a jealous God, who visits the iniquity of fathers on children, even to the third and fourth generations of those who hate me, but who extends faithful love to a thousand generations of those who love me and keep my commandments. You shall not take the name of the LORD your God in vain, for the LORD will not hold guiltless anyone who takes his name in vain. Remember the Sabbath day to sanctify it. For six days you may labor and do all your work, but the seventh day is a Sabbath to the LORD your God; on it you shall not do any work, you, or your son, or your daughter, or your male servant, or your female servant, or your cattle, or your resident foreigner who is in your gates. For in six days the LORD made the heavens and the earth and the sea and all that is in them, and he rested on the seventh day; therefore the LORD blessed the Sabbath day and sanctified it. Honor your father and your mother, that your days may be long in the land the LORD your God is giving to you. You shall not murder. You shall not commit adultery. You shall not steal. You shall not give false testimony against your neighbor. You shall not covet your neighbor's house. You shall not covet your neighbor's wife, nor his male servant, nor his female servant, nor his ox, nor his donkey, nor anything that belongs to your neighbor (Exodus 20:1–17).

Now answer honestly. Have you ever broken one of those laws? *One* is enough to show that you are sinful—a chain broken in *one* link is a broken chain! If one link of an anchor chain breaks, the ship will drift.

Few people are honest enough to admit that they have broken God's laws. There was a young man who claimed that he had faithfully kept all the laws of God. Here is the story: *Now as Jesus was starting out on his way, someone ran up to him, fell on his knees, and said, "Good teacher, what must I do to inherit eternal life?" Jesus said to him, "Why do you call me good? No one is good except God alone. You know the commandments: 'Do not murder, do not commit adultery, do not steal, do not give false testimony, do not defraud, honor your father and mother.'" The man said to him, "Teacher, I have wholeheartedly obeyed all these laws since my youth." As Jesus looked at him, he felt love for him and said, "You lack one thing. Go, sell whatever you have and give the money to the poor, and you will have treasure in heaven. Then come, follow me." But at this statement, the man looked sad and went away sorrowful, for he was very rich* (Mark 10:17–22). This young man did not really understand what he was saying. The mere outward observance of some of God's laws does not prove us to be perfect and holy! Jesus taught this very plainly. He said, *For I tell you, unless your righteousness goes beyond that of the experts in the law and the Pharisees, you will never enter the kingdom of heaven. You have heard that it was said to an older generation, 'Do not murder,' and 'whoever murders will be subjected to judgment.' But I say to you that anyone who is angry with a brother will be subjected to judgment. And whoever insults a brother will be brought before the council, and whoever says 'Fool' will be sent to fiery hell. So then, if you bring your gift to the altar and there remember that your brother has something against you, leave your gift there in front of the altar. First go and be reconciled to your brother and then come and present your gift. Reach agreement quickly with your accuser while on the way to court, or he may hand you over to the judge, and the judge hand you over to the warden, and* you will be thrown into prison. I tell you the truth, you will never get out of there until you have paid the last penny! You have heard that it was said, 'Do not commit adultery.' But I say to you that whoever looks at a woman to desire her has already committed adultery with her in his heart. If your right eye causes you to sin, tear it out and throw it away! It is better to lose one of your members than to have your whole body thrown into hell. If your right hand causes you to sin, cut it off and throw it away! It is better to lose one of your members than to have your whole body go into hell. It was said, 'Whoever divorces his wife must give her a legal document.' But I say to you that everyone who divorces his wife, except for immorality, makes her commit adultery, and whoever marries a divorced woman commits adultery. Again, you have heard that it was said to an older generation, 'Do not break an oath, but fulfill your vows to the Lord.' But I say to you, do not take oaths at all—not by heaven, because it is the throne of God, not by earth, because it is his footstool, and not by Jerusalem, because it is the city of the great King. Do not take an oath by your head, because you are not able to make one hair white or black. Let your word be 'Yes, yes' or 'No, no.' More than this is from the evil one. You have heard that it was said, 'An eye for an eye and a tooth for a tooth.' But I say to you, do not resist the evildoer. But whoever strikes you on the right cheek, turn the other to him as well. And if someone wants to sue you and to take your tunic, give him your coat also. And if anyone forces you to go one mile, go with him two. Give to the one who asks you, and do not reject the one who wants to borrow from you. You have heard that it was said, 'Love your neighbor' and 'hate your enemy.' But I say to you, love your enemy and pray for those who persecute you, so that you may be like your Father in heaven, since he causes the sun to rise on the evil and the good, and sends rain on the righteous and the unrighteous. For if you love those who love you, what reward do you have? Even the tax collectors do the same, don't they? And if you only greet your brothers, what more do you do? Even the Gentiles do the same, don't they? So then, be perfect, as your heavenly Father is perfect (Matthew 5:20–48). You see, not only our outward actions but our inward thoughts and motives are known to God. Jesus said that unless our righteousness exceeds that of the Pharisees, there is no hope of our entering the kingdom of heaven. The Pharisees were Jewish religious leaders who were extremely careful to observe the outward forms of God's laws, but their hearts were full of pride. They would not commit murder or adultery but they were too self-righteous to admit that there was anything lacking in their lives.

Here is another interesting story. *Jesus also told this parable to some who were confident that they were righteous and looked down on everyone else. "Two men went up to the temple to pray, one a Pharisee and the other a tax collector. The Pharisee stood and prayed about himself like this: 'God, I thank you that I am not like other people: extortionists, unrighteous people, adulterers—or even like this tax collector. I fast twice a week; I give a tenth of everything I get.' The tax collector, however, stood far off and would not even look up to heaven, but beat his breast and said, 'God, be merciful to me, sinner that I am!' I tell you that this man went down to his home justified rather than the Pharisee. For everyone who exalts himself will be humbled, but he who humbles himself will be exalted."* (Luke 18:9–14). The Pharisee in this story was so proud of his own good deeds and his outward religious behavior that he actually began to boast to God of his own merit. He made no confession of sin nor did he ask forgiveness from God. The other man, a confessed sinner, prayed to God with humility and asked for forgiveness. Jesus said that the "good" man remained unforgiven by God while the "bad" man was forgiven because of his sincere repentance and humility.

Pride is extremely hateful to God. *The LORD abhors every arrogant person; one can be sure that they will not go unpunished.* (Proverbs 16:5). This is a staggering concept, as we find in Proverbs 6:16–19 where we find a list of seven things which God hates. This list includes murder, lying and other evil things, but the first thing in the list is a "proud heart." Why is this so serious? It is because pride was at the root of the very first human sin, and pride still keeps men and women from humbly confessing their sinfulness to God. God is full of mercy and compassion. No matter how wicked a person may have been He will forgive if that person repents sincerely and asks Him for forgiveness. But pride holds us back! Are you humble enough to admit that you are a sinner in the sight of God? Not just a sinner, but a lost sinner (even though you may consider yourself a very respectable kind of sinner like the religious Pharisee)! Or does pride keep you from true repentance and confession of sin to God? Are you proud of your good living, proud of your diligence in religion, proud of your prayers and fasting? (Remember, the proud Pharisee who was not forgiven, was proud of his fasting and other religious acts.)

No man can afford to be proud in the presence of God; He knows our actions, our thoughts and our motives. The Bible makes it plain that all men are sinners without any exception. Even the greatest and holiest of the prophets confessed their sins to God and found peace and forgiveness through trusting His Word. This is one reason why the Bible tells us so much of the life and history of the great men of faith. It shows us that like all other men they were sinners but they were humble enough to confess their need of salvation, and thus to be forgiven sinners, sinners who became saints, able to enjoy fellowship with God and to serve Him as His messengers. There has been only one exception in the entire history of the human race—Jesus Christ! Notice the contrast in the following verses:

Concerning mankind:

For all have sinned and fall short of the glory of God (Romans 3:23).

Just as it is written: "There is no one righteous, not even one" (Romans 3:10)

"All have turned away, together they have become worthless; there is no one who shows kindness, not even one" (Romans 3:12).

Concerning Jesus Christ:

He committed no sin nor was deceit found in his mouth (1 Peter 2:22).

My little children, I am writing these things to you so that you may not sin. But if anyone does sin, we have an advocate with the Father, Jesus Christ the righteous One (1 John 2:1).

And the one who sent me is with me. He has not left me alone, because I always do those things that please him (John 8:29).

We have seen in a previous chapter that because mankind is sinful, God promised and provided a sinless Savior. But even to this day, because of pride in their hearts, men still reject the good news about a Savior who is Himself sinless.

A drowning man, they tell us, will clutch at a straw. How strange it is that sinners who are in worse danger than a drowning man refuse to seize hold of the only way of salvation. Do you believe that Jesus is the only Savior? Read these words, spoken by the apostle Peter: *And there is salvation in no one else, for there is no other name under heaven given among people by which we must be saved* (Acts 4:12).

CHAPTER TEN

SALVATION FROM SIN

The time has now come to gather together the strands of thought from several earlier chapters. We have studied the teaching of the Bible on the tragic fact of sin in human experience. Sin has so cursed the world, that in spite of all our progress, education, knowledge and religion we still see pride, selfishness, greed, lust, cruelty, violence, hate, war, sorrow and grief wherever we look. Humanism, the belief that man is basically good at heart, has been proved false. The Bible teaching about sin fits in perfectly with the obvious facts of daily experience. We have seen that sin came into human experience through pride, self-will and disobedience to God's laws. We have seen also, that although man is responsible for this awful harvest of misery and sin, God has promised that He will be responsible for the great work of saving us from sin. We have read the promises of a coming Savior so wonderfully foretold by the prophets in detail and so amazingly fulfilled by Jesus Christ that we cannot doubt that He is the revealed Savior of men.

This brings us to a very important question. **How** does Jesus save sinful men and women from their sins and make them fit for eternal life in the presence of God? We have seen that Jesus died and rose from among the dead, but this prompts another question. "**Why** was this necessary? **What** was the purpose of such a tragic death?" We have asked, HOW, WHY, WHAT? We now must look at the Bible to find satisfactory answers to these questions, if we say that Jesus died as a sacrifice, we must find out the meaning of sacrifice, and why only the sacrifice of Jesus can be called a perfect sacrifice. For this we must go back again to the very beginning.

When Adam and Eve disobeyed God, their sin destroyed the perfect communion they had enjoyed with God, for God is holy and He cannot have fellowship with unholy creatures. *For what partnership is there between righteousness and lawlessness, or what fellowship does light have with darkness?* (2 Corinthians 6:14).

Sin separates man from God. *But your sinful acts have alienated you from your God; your sins have caused him to reject you and not listen to your prayers* (Isaiah 59:2). But, even worse, God has said that the penalty for disobedience is death. *But you must not eat from the tree of the knowledge of good and evil, for when you eat from it you will surely die* (Genesis 2:17). God emphatically declares, *The one who sins will die* (Ezekiel 18:4). Notice also the following words, *When sin is full grown, it gives birth to death* (James 1:15). Notice also the statement, *So then, just as sin entered the world through one man and death through sin, and so death spread to all people because all sinned* (Romans 5:12).

Death is said to be the result of sin. What is death? In the Bible death never means cessation of existence. The popular idea is that at death we just "go out like a lamp." The Bible contradicts this. In Scripture, death is spoken of in two ways:

- Physically, death is the separation of the spirit from the body
- Spiritually, death is the separation of the sinner from God.

Both are the result of sin. At the very moment that Adam and Eve sinned, they "died" spiritually—that is they were separated from God; eventually they died physically, when the spirit was separated from the body. Thus, because of sin in human life, the Bible speaks of men and women as being "dead in sins" even while they still live physically. Examine the following quotations:

For the payoff of sin is death, but the gift of God is eternal life in Christ Jesus our Lord (Romans 6:23).

So then, just as sin entered the world through one man and death through sin, and so death spread to all people because all sinned—for before the law was given, sin was in the world, but there is no accounting for sin when there is no law. Yet death reigned from Adam until Moses even over those who did not sin in the same way that Adam (who is a type of the coming one) transgressed. But the gracious gift is not like the transgression. For if the many died through the transgression of the one man, how much more did the grace of God and the gift by the grace of the one man Jesus Christ multiply to the many!

And the gift is not like the one who sinned. For judgment, resulting from the one transgression, led to condemnation, but the gracious gift from the many failures led to justification For if, by the transgression of the one man, death reigned through the one, how much more will those who receive the abundance of grace and of the gift of righteousness reign in life through the one, Jesus Christ! Consequently, just as condemnation for all people came through one transgression, so too through the one righteous act came righteousness leading to life for all people. For just as through the disobedience of the one man many were made sinners, so also through the obedience of one man many will be made righteous. Now the law came in so that the transgression may increase, but where sin increased, grace multiplied all the more, so that just as sin reigned in death, so also grace will reign through righteousness to eternal life through Jesus Christ our Lord (Romans 5:12–21).

And although you were dead in your transgressions and sins, in which you formerly lived according to this world's present path, according to the ruler of the kingdom of the air, the ruler of the spirit that is now energizing the sons of disobedience, among whom all of us also formerly lived out our lives in the cravings of our flesh, indulging the desires of the flesh and the mind, and were by nature children of wrath even as the rest . . . But God, being rich in mercy, because of his great love with which he loved us, even though we were dead in transgressions, made us alive together with Christ—by grace you are saved!—and he raised us up with him and seated us with him in the heavenly realms in Christ Jesus, to demonstrate in the coming ages the surpassing wealth of his grace in kindness toward us in Christ Jesus. For by grace you are saved through faith, and this is not from yourselves, it is the gift of God; it is not from works, so that no one can boast (Ephesians 2:1–9).

But the one who lives for pleasure is dead even while she lives (1 Timothy 5:6).

Now, although sin caused this "spiritual death" (separation from God) God has not ceased to love His creatures. He loves us because that is His character. His plan for man was that man should love, worship and serve God. He therefore planned a way to restore man to fellowship with Himself. This plan was based on the principle of sacrifice. We find this taught plainly in the story of Cain and Abel, the first two men to be born on earth, the sons of Adam and Eve. As grown men, they became responsible to God for their own obedience to God. The story is given here:

> *Now the man had marital relations with his wife Eve, and she became pregnant and gave birth to Cain. Then she said, "I have created a man just as the LORD did!" Then she gave birth to his brother Abel. Abel took care of the flocks, while Cain cultivated the ground. At the designated time Cain brought some of the fruit of the ground for an offering to the LORD. But Abel brought some of the firstborn of his flock—even the fattest of them. And the LORD was pleased with Abel and his offering, but with Cain and his offering he was not pleased. So Cain became very angry, and his expression was downcast. Then the LORD said to Cain, "Why are you angry, and why is your expression downcast? Is it not true that if you do what is right, you will be fine? But if you do not do what is right, sin is crouching at the door. It desires to dominate you, but you must suppress it." Cain said to his brother Abel, "Let's go out to the field." While they were in the field, Cain attacked his brother Abel and killed him* (Genesis 4:1–8).

Now read the comment on this in Hebrews 11:4: *By faith Abel offered God a greater sacrifice than Cain, and through his faith he was commended as righteous, because God commended him for his offerings. And through his faith he still speaks, though he is dead.* Both men believed in God. Both desired to worship Him. Cain brought an offering to God, but it was not a blood sacrifice, and God rejected it. Abel brought a lamb as a sacrifice and God accepted it. Why? Was God unfair? No! God had revealed that only through a blood sacrifice could sinful men approach a holy God, and Cain refused to do this.

From that time onwards every person who desired to worship God in a way that God accepted, offered a blood sacrifice like Abel. Noah, Abraham, Moses, David, Elijah and all the great prophets knew, and taught and practiced the fact that God had commanded the offering of a blood sacrifice to put away their sin. The story of Cain and Abel and all later teaching emphasizes that to offer to God gifts of fruit, money or other things is of no value unless we have first had our sins put away by a blood sacrifice.

The reason for this is clearly given in the words of God Himself —the penalty for sin is death. Because of sin, the sinner must die and be separated from God for ever; but God in His love and wisdom permitted the sinner, in Old Testament times, to offer a substitute to die in his place. To use a modern expression, when a sinner offered a lamb as a sacrifice, it was "death by proxy." Cain objected to this, and millions upon millions up to the present time continue to object. But this was God's plan, not man's. Abel (and millions like him, who accepted God's word, even though they could not understand the reason for God's commands) came in sincere repentance, confessing his sins and offering a blood sacrifice as an act of faith. The blood which flowed when the sacrifice was killed showed vividly that a life had been given as a substitute for the life of the sinner. Because of the faith of the worshipper, God forgave him his sins and restored him to the blessing and favor of God. Thus a sacrifice was evidence of personal faith in God, personal obedience to God, personal repentance and confession of sin.

At the time of Moses, the people of Israel were given a comprehensive Law regarding sacrifices, and the way of true worship. Every day, in the temple of God, lambs were offered in sacrifice to atone for the sins of the people. Now no animal sacrifice could deal adequately and permanently with human sin. So day after day for hundreds of years, countless animal sacrifices were offered at God's command. Now as we have seen in previous lessons, Old Testament prophets were sent to teach many things which would not be fully understood until the coming of the promised Messiah. This was true of the blood sacrifices. When we turn to the New Testament, it all becomes plain. The sacrifices were actually types (pictures or acted parables) pointing forward to one perfect sacrifice, by which God would deal with sin for ever— the sacrifice of Jesus Christ on the cross.

Jesus said, *For even the Son of Man did not come to be served but* to serve, and to give his life as a ransom for many (Mark 10:45). This is explained in the letter to the Hebrews in the following words, *By his will we have been made holy through the offering of the body of Jesus Christ once for all. And every priest stands day after day serving and offering the same sacrifices again and again—sacrifices that can never take away sins. But when this priest had offered one sacrifice for sins for all time, he sat down at the right hand of God* (Hebrews 10:10–12). Many other verses fully support this. Please read the following examples:

> *In him we have redemption through his blood, the forgiveness of our trespasses, according to the riches of his grace* (Ephesians 1:7).

> *In whom we have redemption, the forgiveness of sins* (Colossians 1:14).

> *From Paul, an apostle (not from men, nor by human agency, but by Jesus Christ and God the Father who raised him from the dead) and all the brothers with me, to the churches of Galatia. Grace and peace to you from God the Father and our Lord Jesus Christ, who gave himself for our sins to rescue us from this present evil age according to the will of our God and Father* (Galatians 1:1–4).

Jesus was sinless. He did not forfeit His life as sinful men do; He was therefore able to come willingly and offer His sinless life as a perfect sacrifice for sinful men. John, one of the greatest of the prophets, pointed to Jesus and said to his listeners, *Look, the Lamb of God who takes away the sin of the world!* (John 1:29). But did He give His life willingly? Oh yes! He says so Himself, *I am the good shepherd. The good shepherd lays down his life for the sheep. . . . This is why the Father loves me—because I lay down my life, so that I may take it back again. No one takes it away from me, but I lay it down of my own free will. I have the authority to lay it down, and I have the authority to take it back again* (John 10:11, and 17–18). It is true that the Jews demanded His death and the Romans carried out the execution, but Jesus Himself declared they would have had no power at all against Him unless He had given Himself willingly to die.

Jesus was not compelled to die. Because of His love for us, He took our place and died as our sacrifice to atone for our sins. The blood which flowed from His body was the proof that the penalty of sin had been paid—the ultimate penalty, death. At this point a question arises in the minds of many people, if Jesus died as a substitute for sinners, why do Christians die? If death is the result of sin, then why should people die if their sins are forgiven? This takes us back to the beginning again! God did not promise to reverse at once the penalty of physical death, or as we saw, the separation of the spirit from the body. That penalty still remains in force. But what God did promise to deal with at once was "spiritual death"—the separation of the sinner from God forever. When sin is forgiven, God gives to the believer "eternal life" which means that nothing now separates the believer in Christ from fellowship with God. And when the Day of Resurrection comes the dead will be raised; then body and spirit will be re-united and thus the complete person will enter into the presence of God forever.

God has said that the perfect sacrifice of Jesus Christ has made an end of all other sacrifices. All the Old Testament sacrifices became obsolete upon the death of Christ. Just a few short years after Jesus died and rose from among the dead, the Romans destroyed Jerusalem and its temple. Since then, no Jew has been able to offer a blood sacrifice to God. God's law permitted them to sacrifice only in the Temple and nowhere else on earth.

With this long explanation of the meaning of sacrifices in the Old Testament and the explanation of how they came to an end in the New Testament, we ask the question, "How can a sinner be saved from the penalty of his sins today?" Actually, the way of salvation is the same as in the past. Let us read what David the prophet said in Psalm 32:5: *Then I confessed my sin; I no longer covered up my wrongdoing. I said, "I will confess my rebellious acts to the LORD." And then you forgave my sins.* David uses three descriptive words to confess his spiritual needs. He humbly confessed his wrongdoing, his rebellion and his sin. This is the first step in the way of salvation. We must make a sincere confession of our sins to God. This includes confessing that our nature is perverted, that our behavior is rebellious, and that in all things we have failed to reach God's standard of holiness. Repentance is not just a glib admission that we have been found out! Repentance is a realization that we have sinned against God, and our sin is an offense to Him. He loves us and desires us to be holy; therefore, there must be a desire in our hearts to be saved from our sins. David the prophet prayed to God to *cleanse his sin* (Psalm 51:2) and to create in him *a pure heart* (Psalm 51:10). Unless our repentance and confession is sincere, God cannot accept our prayers or worship, or even accept a sacrifice from us. David points out this very fact later on in the same Psalm. In other words, David realized that even though God had commanded sacrifices, it was useless for him to offer them unless he intended to turn away from his sin.

The only sacrifice God accepts today is the perfect and final sacrifice of Jesus on the cross. When a sinner truly repents and trusts in God to forgive his sin because of what Jesus has done, God immediately forgives him and sets him free from the penalty. He receives "eternal life"!

Are you willing to accept Jesus Christ as your Sacrifice and your Savior? This is the most important question you will ever be asked to decide in your lifetime.

Possibly your immediate reaction is "I cannot understand all this!" God does not expect us to understand it but because it is His will, to accept it by faith. We are not saved from sin by our intellectual grasp of this Divine plan but by simple, personal trust in what God has said. This can be summed up in a few words:

- God now commands all men everywhere to repent (see Acts 17:30).
- God recommends His love to us in that Christ died for our sins (see Romans 5:8).
- God asks us to believe what He has said. *For what does the scripture say? "Abraham believed God, and it was credited to him as righteousness."* (Romans 4:3).

Are you willing to repent, to believe in Jesus Christ's death as a sacrifice for sin, and to trust Him as your Savior?

CHAPTER ELEVEN

RELIGION OR SALVATION

This is a strange title for our next chapter! Most people think that salvation is found in religion. The Bible does not say so! Notice also, we did not say "other religions" as if the Christian religion were different. There are millions of people who claim to be following the "Christian religion" but they are not really followers of Christ at all!

Anyone who reads the New Testament carefully will realize that Jesus did not come to found a religion. The Jewish religion had been given by God at the time of Moses (1500 B.C.) and its main purpose was to prepare the way for the coming of the Savior. Jesus came into the world to save sinners, which is a very different thing from founding a religion.

To illustrate this point, let us think for a moment of the religion of Islam. Islam is a religion which has a comprehensive Law (Shariah) which regulates every aspect of the life of Muslim peoples. This Law is so detailed that Islam is actually a religious system, **and** a legal system, **and** a political system **and** a social system. Islamic Law covers religion, ethics, marriage, divorce, inheritance, diet, dress, taxation and similar matters and in the fullest sense it can only be practiced ideally in an Islamic State. Islam is thus a religion, a culture and a community in which Muslim life is governed by the laws of the Quran and the Traditions. In contrast with this, no rules are given in the New Testament for a religious-state-culture system to be embraced by the followers of Christ. This is a startling concept to many people.

Jesus said that He came to *build my church* (Matthew 16:18) which would consist of all those who trusted and obeyed Him as Savior. The State is mentioned in the New Testament. Christians are viewed as a minority in the State which is more often than not hostile to them. (This is not really part of our main subject, but the student can check up for his own interest by reading the following sample references:

Romans 13:1–10; 1 Peter 2:11–17; Acts 4:1–3; Acts 8:1–3; Acts 12:1–5; Acts 16:22–24.)

Millions of people equate Christianity with Western Civilization. Many think that Christianity and Capitalism are the same thing. Such an idea is completely foreign to the Bible. It is true that many lands in the West have adopted the basic ideals and ethics of the gospel and have thus become known as "Christian nations" but this is only a cultural development. From the very first time the gospel of Christ was proclaimed, its message was clearly one of spiritual truth, completely and entirely non-cultural! One of the reasons for the initial hostility of the Jewish leaders toward Christianity was because the Christians disregarded cultural and racial ties completely. Greeks, Romans, Jews, and peoples of many tribes and nations were brought together in a new brotherhood of equality and unity. Slaves and their masters, aristocrats and commoners, soldiers and their officers, all shared the common life of the church of Christ. All were permitted to retain their own cultural heritage except for those customs which were tainted by idolatry or immorality. An example of this is given in Acts 15:28–29:

> *"For it seemed best to the Holy Spirit and to us not to place any greater burden on you than these necessary rules: that you abstain from meat that has been sacrificed to idols and from blood and from what has been strangled and from sexual immorality. If you keep yourselves from doing these things, you will do well. Farewell.*

True followers of Christ have always been a minority group. Jesus and His disciples were a "little flock" within the Jewish circle. Christians were a minority in Greek or Roman cities; they are still a minority, in the world today, whether in Asia, in Africa or in European lands. In England, for example, less than 10% of the people ever attend any form of religious service yet people think of England as a "Christian" country! In many countries the Christians are a very small minority. What then, is the advantage of being a Christian? Why choose a "religion" which does not even offer the benefit of a common, unifying culture and the security of communal strength?

This is the reason—the gospel offers us personal salvation from sin! Men are not saved from sin in communities, but as individuals who realize that they are personally responsible to God. "Religion" can indeed be a cohesive force in social, communal and national affairs. The gospel of Christ emphasizes the vital importance of the individual and the great responsibility each person has to decide for himself the all-important matter of salvation from sin. This is evident from the very beginning in the teaching of Jesus Christ Himself. When He first began to preach, vast crowds flocked to hear Him, attracted by His personality, His teaching and His miracles. They imagined He would soon dominate the religious and political life of Israel and bring in "the golden age" of Jewish universal sovereignty. But as they heard His unchanging emphasis on the moral issues of sin and repentance, the majority of His "followers" deserted Him. An example of this is given in John 6:66–69. As Jesus watched the crowds turning away from Him, He said to His disciples, *You don't want to go away too, do you.* The apostle Peter replied, *Lord, to whom would we go? You have the words of eternal life. We have come to believe and to know that you are the Holy One of God!* Peter was absolutely right! Those who are seeking religion, or culture, or pleasure, or security can find many leaders to follow—leaders who make no heart-searching demands for confession of sin and sincere repentance. But if we want eternal life, there is no alternative! It is Christ or nothing! Read the following words of Jesus:

> *But the gate is narrow and the way is difficult that leads to life, and there are few who find it* (Matthew 7:14).

> *Jesus replied, "I am the way, and the truth, and the life. No one comes to the Father except through me"* (John 14:6).

Read also the words of the apostle Peter. *And there is salvation in no one else, for there is no other name under heaven given among people by which we must be saved* (Acts 4:12).

It is at this point that we realize that the Bible is different from all books. Every religion in the world has as its base the idea that we must try to atone for our own sins, and that we can acquire merit by good deeds and religious acts. The way of "salvation" in "religion" is through human merit; through the good deeds balancing up the bad deeds. Islam, for example, lays great stress on the importance of ritual prayers, prescribed fasts, pilgrimages, alms giving and other religious acts by means of which the faithful are promised Paradise.

The gospel is totally different! God says that we are sinful and that no merits of our own can deal with this fatal spiritual condition. No human merit can change the deadly harvest of sin. In Galatians 6:7–8 we read *Do not be deceived. God will not be made a fool. For a person will reap what he sows, because the person who sows to his own flesh will reap corruption from the flesh, but the one who sows to the Spirit will reap eternal life from the Spirit.* Our problem is that we have a sinful nature and we *cannot please God* (Romans 8:8). The popular notion is that if we try to do as many good things as possible then God will balance this against our sins and will forgive us! This false idea arises from a failure to understand how truly holy God is and how far we have come short of His standard. The Bible says, *all have sinned and fall short of the glory of God"* (Romans 3:23).

Suppose a businessman decided to pay half of his debts and ignore the rest of his liabilities! Would he be being honest or dishonest? Would the "merit" of his paying off half his debts atone for his failure to pay the other half? Of course not! His clear obligation is to pay off all that he owes. Religious people think that by being good and kind and honest and moral they can somehow accumulate merit and that this merit can be used to pay off their liability of sin. But these things are all obligations; we ought to do these things all the time. Since being good and kind, moral and honest is what God demands of us as life's standard of behavior it is obvious we cannot offer Him half payment and say "Yesterday I failed to do and be all that you demand. I think I did better today. Please accept today's achievement in payment for yesterday's failure." His answer would be, "You should have done and been all that I expected both yesterday and today." In any case we cannot live the kind of life that God demands; when we sin we are simply showing our inability to live up to the standard of goodness that God requires of us. Read the following verses:

And although you were dead in your transgressions and sins, in which you formerly lived according to this world's present path, according to the ruler of the kingdom of the air, the ruler of the spirit that is now energizing the sons of disobedience, among whom all of us also formerly lived out our lives in the cravings of our flesh, indulging the desires of the flesh and the mind, and were by nature children of wrath even as the rest . . . But God, being rich in mercy, because of his great love with which he loved us, even though we were dead in transgressions, made us alive together with Christ—by grace you are saved!—and he raised us up with him and seated us with him in the heavenly realms in Christ Jesus, to demonstrate in the coming ages the surpassing wealth of his grace in kindness toward us in Christ Jesus. For by grace you are saved through faith, and this is not from yourselves, it is the gift of God; it is not from works, so that no one can boast (Ephesians 2:1–9).

Yet we know that no one is justified by the works of the law but by the faithfulness of Jesus Christ. And we have come to believe in Christ Jesus, so that we may be justified by the faithfulness of Christ and not by the works of the law, because by the works of the law no one will be justified (Galatians 2:16).

But when the kindness of God our Savior and his love for mankind appeared, he saved us not by works of righteousness that we have done but on the basis of his mercy, through the washing of the new birth and the renewing of the Holy Spirit, whom he poured out on us in full measure through Jesus Christ our Savior. And so, since we have been justified by his grace, we become heirs with the confident expectation of eternal life (Titus 3:4–7).

The Bible tells us that no matter how popular and appealing the notion of human merit and religious good deeds might be, this path leads to hell. It is a broad way, crowded with lost people vainly hoping they will reach heaven at the end of life's journey. But just because the great mass of humanity is going in that fatal direction is no reason why we should blindly follow them! This is the very heart of the gospel message. Each person is individually accountable to God; each person is responsible for his own repentance and confession of sin, for his own personal faith in Jesus Christ as Savior. Jesus said, *Listen! I am standing at the door and knocking! If anyone hears my voice and opens the door I will come into his home and share a meal with him, and he with me* (Revelation 3:20). He said, *But to all who have received him—those who believe in his name—he has given the right to become God's children* (John 1:12). Paul said, *If anyone is in Christ, he is a new creation* (2 Corinthians 5:17). In all these verses the dominant note is personal acceptance of Christ, personal faith and personal commitment to Christ as Savior and Lord. Have you made a personal decision to accept Jesus Christ as your Savior?

CHAPTER TWELVE

LIVING THE LIFE

We have seen that salvation is a personal experience based on a personal trust in Jesus Christ as Lord and Savior—quite different from observing the rituals of a religion. **Personal** repentance, **personal** faith and **personal** obedience are essential facts of the gospel; however, being a Christian is not a "lone wolf" experience. The very reverse is true, for the new Christian finds himself at once in a new "family" called the "church" which consists of all true followers of Christ everywhere.

Many people are attracted to the gospel because it guarantees assurance of eternal life through Christ; they hesitate, however, to take the step of faith because they are uncertain about the impact being a Christian will have on the daily life. There is a sense of fear, like a man might have who has to take a leap in the dark without knowing what lies ahead. All this is very understandable so in this lesson we shall look at some aspects of the problem. After his personal decision to receive Christ as Savior, the "new" Christian has an instinctive desire for the company of other Christians. This is why Christians so often engage in united activities. They have a spontaneous desire to praise God in singing and public worship. From the very beginning of the Christian church, hymns of praise have been sung; today thousands of hymns in scores of languages are used wherever Christians meet together. Now let us examine some of the essential features of daily Christian life.

PRAYER

Prayer is as natural to a true Christian as breathing! Just as the air we breathe is necessary for life, so prayer, the link between our souls and God, maintains our spiritual lives in a healthy state. But what form does Christian prayer take? The Bible does not prescribe ritual prayers. A Christian may pray to God in any language (it is not necessary to use a "sacred language") for true prayer comes from the heart. A Christian may speak to God as a child or a son speaks to his father. When

Jesus taught His disciples to pray, He said, *So pray this way: Our Father in heaven, may your name be honored, may your kingdom come, may your will be done on earth as it is in heaven. Give us today our daily bread, and forgive us our debts, as we ourselves have forgiven our debtors. And do not lead us into temptation, but deliver us from the evil one* (Matthew 6:9–13). God is not a remote unknowable Being, but a loving, gracious Father to His children on earth. A Christian may pray in secret, with his family or as part of his public worship. Here are some Bible verses on prayer:

> *When they had entered Jerusalem, they went to the upstairs room where they were staying. Peter and John, and James, and Andrew, Philip and Thomas, Bartholomew and Matthew, James son of Alphaeus and Simon the Zealot, and Judas son of James were there. All these continued together in prayer with one mind, together with the women, along with Mary the mother of Jesus, and his brothers (Acts 1:13–14).*

> *They were devoting themselves to the apostles' teaching and to fellowship, to the breaking of bread and to prayer . . . . praising God and having the good will of all the people. And the Lord was adding to their number every day those who were being saved (Acts 2:42 and 47).*

> *So Peter was kept in prison, but those in the church were earnestly praying to God for him (Acts 12:5).*

> *Do not be anxious about anything. Instead, in every situation, through prayer and petition with thanksgiving, tell your requests to God (Philippians 4:6).*

> *First of all, then, I urge that requests, prayers, intercessions, and thanks be offered on behalf of all people, even for kings and all who are in authority, that we may lead a peaceful and quiet life in all godliness and dignity. Such prayer for all is good and welcomed before God our Savior (1 Timothy 2:1–3).*

BIBLE READING

The Bible is the Christian's source of authority, guidance and instruction. Therefore every Christian should read the Bible daily and meditate on its meaning. There is no merit in reading the Bible in its original language unless we understand its meaning. Parts of the Bible have been translated into thousands of languages so most people can read it in their mother-tongue. Reading the Bible is like partaking of spiritual food; it sustains and builds up spiritual life just as ordinary food sustains physical life. In the Bible instruction is given on all the important matters of life. Study of the Bible may be a private and personal exercise; it may be something the family does together; or it may take the form of the public teaching of its truths. A Christian may read, study and learn without the help of a religious teacher or priest. Where capable Bible teachers are available, however, we can gain great help from their knowledge and experience.

COLLECTIVE WORSHIP

When Christians meet for prayer, worship or Bible study, no special or sacred buildings are necessary. They may meet together in homes, in schools or, if no other convenient place is to be found, they may meet in the open air.

FESTIVALS OR HOLY DAYS

The New Testament gives no rules for the observance of holy days. Throughout the world certain days are now set aside as religious days. (particularly Christmas and Easter), but the observance of these is not an obligatory aspect of the gospel. There is no merit in observing them, nor is there any de-merit in ignoring them. Christians can take advantage of these public holidays (which are in reality cultural festivals—encrusted with myths and exploited by commercialism) to emphasize the vital truths concerning the birth and death and resurrection of Christ, which are often neglected by the masses. Although there is no command to observe any particular day of the week for worship (every day is holy when we love the Lord and seek to please Him in our daily lives) yet it was the custom of the early Christians to meet for worship on the first day of the week, and this is still the normal practice. The first day was loved by the disciples because it was on this day that Jesus rose from the dead; it was on the first day of the week also that the Holy Spirit was given (Acts 2). A Christian in a non-Christian community may have no opportunity to observe Sunday in this way. He does not have to feel that he is failing in his religious duty!

PILGRIMAGES

The New Testament does not require pilgrimage of any kind, to any place. To the Christian, every place is blessed by the presence of God. It is true that millions of people make "pilgrimages" to so-called "holy places" in the Middle East and elsewhere, but this is simply custom and is not part of the essential teaching of the Bible. On the contrary, it is often mere superstitious veneration of sacred places and is quite contrary to the teaching of Christ. Some Christians do visit the Bible lands as tourists to gain first-hand knowledge of Biblical backgrounds and to see the places where Christ lived, died and rose again. Such expeditions are not compulsory or obligatory.

FOOD LAWS

No laws concerning diet are given in the New Testament except that Christians must not participate at idol feasts. *For it seemed best to the Holy Spirit and to us not to place any greater burden on you than these necessary rules: that you abstain from meat that has been sacrificed to idols and from blood and from what has been strangled and from sexual immorality. If you keep yourselves from doing these things, you will do well. Farewell (Acts 15:28–29). Am I saying that idols or food sacrificed to them amount to anything? No, I mean that what the pagans sacrifice is to demons and not to God. I do not want you to be partners with demons. You cannot drink the cup of the Lord and the cup of demons. You cannot take part in the table of the Lord and the table of demons. Or are we trying to provoke the Lord to jealousy? Are we really stronger than he is? "Everything is lawful," but not everything is beneficial. "Everything is lawful," but not everything builds others up. Do not seek your own good, but the good of the other person. Eat anything that is sold in the marketplace without questions of conscience, for the earth and its abundance are the Lord's. If an unbeliever invites you to dinner and you want to go, eat whatever is served without asking questions of conscience. But if someone says to you, "This is from a sacrifice," do not eat, because of the one who told you and because of conscience— I do not mean yours but the other person's. For why is my freedom being judged by another's conscience? If I partake with thankfulness, why am I blamed for the food that I give thanks for? So whether you eat or drink, or whatever you do, do everything for the glory of God. Do not give offense to Jews or Greeks or to the church of God, just as I also try to please everyone in all things. I do not seek my own benefit, but the benefit of many, so that they may be saved.* (1 Corinthians 10:19–33). Jesus taught that no food defiles a man; it is sin which makes a person unclean.

> *Then he called the crowd again and said to them, "Listen to me, everyone, and understand. There is nothing outside of a person that can defile him by going into him. Rather, it is what comes out of a person that defiles him." Now when Jesus had left the crowd and entered the house, his disciples asked him about the parable. He said to them, "Are you so foolish? Don't you understand that whatever goes into a person from outside cannot defile him? For it does not enter his heart but his stomach, and then goes out into the sewer." (This means all foods are clean.) He said, "What comes out of a person defiles him. For from within, out of the human heart, come evil ideas, sexual immorality, theft, murder, adultery, greed, evil, deceit, debauchery, envy, slander, pride, and folly. All these evils come from within and defile a person"* (Mark 7:14–23).

MARRIAGE

Christian marriage sets a very high ideal. *Marriage must be honored among all and the marriage bed kept undefiled* (Hebrews 13:4). Christians are to be monogamous—a man is to have only one wife, to whom he is married until parted by death. Divorce is not permitted except for adultery (Matthew 5:32). The widespread increase in the divorce rate in Western lands is not an indication of laxity among

Christian people as many think. On the contrary, it is an indication of the extent to which modern society has rejected the teaching of the Bible.

DEATH

For Christians, death is not a hopeless tragedy. The assurance of eternal life takes the sting out of death, although there is still the natural grief at the loss of those we love. The certainty of the resurrection makes death just a temporary parting for those who are true Christians. *"Now when this perishable puts on the imperishable, and this mortal puts on immortality, then the saying that is written will happen, 'Death has been swallowed up in victory.' 'Where, O death, is your victory? Where, O death, is your sting?' The sting of death is sin, and the power of sin is the law. But thanks be to God, who gives us the victory through our Lord Jesus Christ! So then, dear brothers and sisters, be firm. Do not be moved! Always be outstanding in the work of the Lord, knowing that your labor is not in vain in the Lord* (1 Corinthians 15:54–58). Christians ought not to have elaborate funerals, nor should they practice extensive mourning rites. The Bible teaches plainly that there is no virtue, merit or purpose in praying for the dead. No after-death ritual is practiced by genuine Christians. Normally, the body is buried with a simple ceremony consisting of Bible reading and prayers for the comfort of the sorrowing relatives. The Bible teaches that the body is simply a "house of clay" in which the precious soul lives. Extravagant expenditure at funerals is therefore a waste of money and contrary to the teaching of Scripture. Any Christian may conduct burial services—the presence of an official religious leader or priest is not required, provided all that is done is in keeping with the law of the land.

WITNESSING TO OTHER PEOPLE

Every Christian is a servant of God. He has an obligation to his Lord to tell other people about salvation through Christ. Witness to Christ can be the simple act of telling someone else how Jesus Christ has forgiven our sins, or it can be the public preaching of the gospel. The method may vary according to circumstances but the basic fact is that every Christian is a representative of Christ.

CHRISTIAN MORAL STANDARDS

The Old Testament and the New Testament teaching both give a simple definition of the moral standard God requires of men. Here it is, *You are to be holy because I am holy.* See Leviticus 11:45 and 1 Peter 1:15–16. Because God is holy, His followers and worshippers should strive to be like Him. The teaching of Christianity sets a higher moral standard than is to be found anywhere else in the world. A Christian may not attain to the standard set by the life of Christ who did no sin, in thought, word or deed; but He is the believer's Example just the same. We should pray for strength to be like Him. To acquire some knowledge of the ethics of the Bible, begin by reading Ephesians 5 and 6 and Colossians 3 and 4.

BAPTISM

Christian baptism is not a mystical initiation rite by which a person is somehow converted to the Christian faith. It is a public confession of the faith by which the convert has already become a child of God and a follower of Christ.

You will observe that, in all aspects of the Christian life, the central feature of the gospel is the **personal** aspect. Every individual person is important to God. God is not interested merely in communities, tribes, races, or religious groups; He has revealed His great love for each individual human being. Thus to be a Christian, a person must personally trust Christ as His Savior, and personally seek to glorify God by his daily life. As an individual a Christian prays for guidance and reads the Bible for his spiritual food; as an individual he asks the Holy Spirit to teach him the will of God day by day. This is very different from being part of a communal religion where personal identity is submerged in communal patterns of behavior. A Christian may live alone, without any other Christian and deprived of the joy of collective worship and service yet, on a personal level, enjoy fellowship with God and fulfill all the essential practices of the Christian faith.

In this chapter, we have touched on the most elementary aspects of these subjects. You can continue your study of these things by reading your Bible and, possibly, by obtaining other Emmaus courses.